Presentations That Persuade and Motivate

The Results-Driven Manager Series

The Results-Driven Manager series collects timely articles from *Harvard Management Update* and *Harvard Management Communication Letter* to help senior to middle managers sharpen their skills, increase their effectiveness, and gain a competitive edge. Presented in a concise, accessible format to save managers valuable time, these books offer authoritative insights and techniques for improving job performance and achieving immediate results.

Other books in the series:

Managing Yourself for the Career You Want

Teams That Click

Face-to-Face Communications for Clarity and Impact

Winning Negotiations That Preserve Relationships

A Timesaving Guide

THE RESULTS-DRIVEN MANAGER

Presentations That Persuade and Motivate

• • •

Harvard Business School Press

Boston, Massachusetts

Printed in the United States of America
08 07   5 4

978-1-59139-349-8 (ISBN 13)

Library of Congress Cataloging-in -Publication Data

The results-driven manager: presentations that persuade and motivate.
       p.   cm. — (The results-driven manager series)
    Added t.p. title: Presentations that persuade and motivate.
    Includes bibliographical references and index.
    ISBN 1-59139-349-3
    1. Business presentations. 2. Oral communication. 3. Public
speaking. 4. Business communication. I. Title: Presentations that
persuade and motivate. II. Series.
    HF5718.22.R47 2004
    658.4'52—dc22

                                            2003020746

Contents

Contents

Delivering Your Presentation

Strengthening Your Presentation with Powerful Tools and Techniques

Presentations That Persuade and Motivate

Introduction

. . .

That moment you've been dreading has come: You have to make a presentation to a group. Already, your stomach is churning and your palms are sweaty. How will you get through this experience? It helps to realize that you're not alone. Many people—even the most accomplished public speakers—feel everything from slight nervousness to outright terror before they give a presentation. In fact, one study revealed that an alarmingly high number of people would rather have unnecessary surgery than give a speech!

But despite the butterflies-in-the-stomach sensation, you *can* take steps to prepare for and deliver a successful, memorable presentation. The trick isn't to try to vanquish your nervousness; instead, it's to "get all those butterflies flying in formation" (as they say in the public-speaking trade). By following some basic but powerful guidelines, you can transform nervousness into a positive energy that infuses all your presentations—and gets you the results you want.

Are you thinking, "All this sounds like it requires a lot of time—and I don't have that luxury"? If so, consider this: The ability to give effective presentations isn't just a "luxury" skill to acquire—it's becoming increasingly essential in the business world. Even though we're living in an age of technology, face-to-face human communication is still the preferred vehicle for learning and sharing our ideas and insights. More and more, managers are being asked to make presentations to audiences ranging from their own direct reports and other managers to supervisors, customers, and industry colleagues. A manager who can be counted on to deliver effective presentations stands a far better chance of advancing in his or her career than one who doesn't bother to master this essential art.

If you need more persuading, think about presentations *you've* attended that turned out to be awful. You know—that talk in which the speaker droned on for what seemed like hours, and you barely managed to keep your eyes open. Or the one where the presenter just raced through a series of PowerPoint slides filled with tiny, unreadable text. Though both of these disasters may have had a different twist, they shared one thing: The presenters wasted their audiences' and their own time—and their companies' money.

Convinced? Good—you're ready to take your first steps down the path to becoming a powerful presenter. The secrets to successful presentations are simple:

- **PREPARATION**—clarifying your purpose, understanding your audience, structuring your presentation to meet your audience's needs, and managing stage fright.

- **DELIVERY**—capturing your listeners' attention at the outset of your speech, holding it throughout the rest of your presentation, and then deftly handling the Q&A at the end of your talk.

To that end, we've organized the articles in this collection into three broad categories:

- Preparing Your Presentation

- Delivering Your Presentation

- Strengthening Your Presentation with Powerful Tools and Techniques

Though you're welcome to peruse the volume's selections in any order, you might want to tackle them sequentially if you're new to public speaking or particularly daunted by the thought of giving a presentation. If you decide to read the articles in the order shown here, you'll consider the challenges of preparation first.

Preparing for Your Presentation

What's Your Purpose? As the articles in this section confirm, there are many different *kinds* of presentations—each of which has a different purpose. Think about that upcoming talk you have to give. What's its purpose? Do you need to deliver bad news to your department? Call for a decision from your superiors on a thorny business matter? Propose a solution to that nagging problem of high staff turnover in your unit?

Or is your presentation supposed to *persuade* your listeners to buy into your ideas—and to inspire your audience so much that they're *motivated* to take action? For example, will you be trying to close a big sale? Launch a major change effort? Get the board to approve a risky new investment? According to Nick Morgan in "The Three Toughest Presentations," persuasive and motivating presentations count among the most challenging public-speaking efforts in the business world. "Speeches like these," Morgan writes, "require more finesse." They're a lot more crucial than merely "talking frankly about a product delay to an irate user group" or "analyzing some poor third-quarter numbers in front of a skeptical pack of Wall Street number-crunchers."

Indeed, presentations that persuade and motivate are becoming increasingly important in companies everywhere. Why? The business world is changing faster than ever—with new technologies upending old business

models, customer tastes changing with little or no warn-
ing, surprising new competitors looming on the horizon, and unprecedented global dynamics rewriting the
old rules of international commerce. Managers who can
make presentations that persuade listeners to face—and
respond to—such changes bring a much-needed skill to
their companies.

Persuasive and motivating presentations are important for another reason, too. Many large organizations
have adopted a flatter management structure—in which
managers must get things done by collaborating with
others over whom they have no formal authority. And
the concept of employee empowerment has caught the
attention of many companies that want to see workers
participating in more decision making. Simply put, it's
the rare manager today who can order people around
and expect them to obey mindlessly.

So, you have to persuade people to change the way
they do things in the workplace. But don't assume that
you can just let the facts speak for themselves when
you're proposing a new course of action. As Morgan
explains in "Build a Presentation That Motivates":

> Your presentation needs to lead your audience
> through [decision-making steps]. Your audience
> needs to go through the decision-making process
> journey with you. Unless they own the decision,
> they won't act on it.

And as the ancient Roman rhetorician Quintilian pragmatically noted, "A mediocre speech supported by all the power of delivery will be more impressive than the best speech unaccompanied by such power." In short, a persuasive delivery packs a far more powerful punch than a factually correct presentation utterly lacking in motivational quality.

Who's Your Audience? When you're preparing to deliver a persuasive and motivating presentation, it's easy to believe that the upcoming speech is all about you and your ideas. It isn't: It's about your listeners. Before you can figure out exactly what you're going to say, you need to think about who your audience is—and what they'll require from you in order to buy into your argument.

Michael Hattersley, in "The Key to Making Better Presentations: Audience Analysis," describes seven ways you can peer into your intended audience's hearts and minds *before* you start crafting your presentation. And speaking of audiences, you'll likely have more than one. Your audience doesn't consist solely of the people who will be sitting before you while you talk—i.e., the key decision makers. It's any group that might possibly be influenced or affected by your proposal—such as teams whose jobs may be made more difficult thanks to your proposal and individuals who might exert some influence over the decision makers in the future.

In addition to defining your various audiences, Hattersley offers a range of recommendations—from deciding what approach is most appropriate for your primary audience (will you *tell* them to do something? *ask* them?) and anticipating their attitude toward your proposal, to assessing how much they already know about what you'll be saying and selling the benefits (not the features) of your proposal.

How Should You Structure Your Presentation? You've clarified your purpose and analyzed your audience. Now it's time to figure out how you'll structure your presentation. What will you say first? second? third? How will you wrap up your talk? In "Build a Presentation That Motivates," Morgan takes a closer look at how to walk your listeners through the decision-making journey you want them to travel.

Morgan recommends beginning with a brief story that reveals the problem at hand—and speaks to your audience's concerns. For example:

> You might relate a conversation you had with a
> disappointed Wall Street analyst who was thinking
> about downgrading your [company's] stock. That
> will work well if your employees have some equity
> in the company.

Follow up your story with an honest analysis of the problematic situation. Then present the good part: your solution. Spell out the benefits of the solution you're proposing, then give your listeners an easy-to-achieve step (creating a to-do list, identifying exciting opportunities for their department) that they can take immediately to start garnering the benefits you've described so enticingly.

For a compelling example of how this process worked in a famous historical speech, be sure to read "How to Structure a Persuasive Speech." This article maps the sections of Abraham Lincoln's Gettysburg Address—which comprised just 250 words and took roughly two minutes to deliver—onto the process Morgan describes.

How Will You Manage Those Butterflies? As a final step in preparing your presentation, you can also take steps to control stage fright. In fact, it's a good idea to deal with nervousness during the preparation stage. As John Daly and Isa Engleberg explain in "Coping with Stage Fright," you can certainly use techniques to control stage fright *during* a talk. However, particularly nervous speakers may find it easier to tackle those butterflies during the preparation stage.

To that end, Daly and Engleberg describe a wealth of handy strategies for reducing jitters before you walk onto the stage to that podium. Merely understanding your audience and your material, they argue, is a powerful first step. The more you know about your listeners and your topic, the more confidence you'll feel on stage—and nothing dispels nervousness faster than confidence. These authors even recommend memorizing the first minute of your presentation. Why? Most people experience the worst anxiety at the outset of giving a speech. By memorizing those first 60 seconds, you'll help yourself over that hump.

Delivering Your Presentation

You've carefully prepared your presentation—clarifying your purpose, analyzing your audience, deciding how to structure your talk, and managing stage fright. What are some things you can do *during* your delivery to boost your chances of getting the results you desire? The article "Are Your Presentations Inspiring?" in the second section sets the stage by providing an overview of effective techniques. Using President John F. Kennedy's address to the citizens of West Berlin on June 26, 1963—a speech that created a sensation among Kennedy's listeners—the article lays out basic but potent guidelines. For example, stick to one main theme as you're talking, repeat a memorable phrase often, and appeal to noble principles that go beyond your audience's self-interest.

Grab Your Listeners' Attention . . . In that all-important first 60 seconds of your talk, you can also take steps to capture your audience's attention. Follow the advice of the authors of "Six Ways to Grab Your Audience Right from the Start" and "Five Winning Ways to Begin a Presentation" and try to resist the conventional wisdom that says the best way to start a talk is with a one-liner. The number of people who can reliably pull this off is very small. The fact is, good jokes are "hard to find, harder still to deliver, and quick to expire."

So what should you do instead to open your presentation with a bang? Relate a personal account of how you came to be involved in the topic at hand. Throw out a quirky fact. Ask a probing, provocative question. These authors provide a rich array of options to choose from— as well as numerous examples from actual speeches.

. . . Then Hold *It* It's not enough to captivate your listeners at the outset of your speech—you also have to *maintain* their attention throughout the rest of the presentation. In "Are You Listening to Me?" Richard Bierck describes effective techniques for analyzing listeners' body language to see whether they're still tuned in—and then "waking them up" if they're not. The key is to get your audience actively involved in your talk. For instance, ask for a show of hands on a practice or opinion—then use the "votes" as a springboard for further discussion and questions. Also, identify an especially attentive member of the audience, and develop a nonverbal rapport with him or her through eye contact and smiling. "When you 'catch' someone not listening," Bierck recommends, "make him the new person you are relating to. Perhaps other nonlisteners will come along."

Judith Humphrey adds to Bierck's advice in "You Are the Best Visual." In Humphrey's view, you don't need PowerPoint slides to hold your listeners' attention throughout a presentation. You just need . . . you! Humphrey points out that the greatest speeches in human history—JFK's inaugural address, Margaret Thatcher's Falkland Islands address, Martin Luther King, Jr.'s "I Have a Dream" speech—did *not* include visual aids. So how do talented presenters keep their audiences tuned in without graphics? They focus listeners' attention on *them*—by walking or sitting among the audience, holding their heads high, and using gestures to underscore a point. By emphasizing your physical presence, you prompt your audience to concentrate on you visually—increasing the likelihood that you'll get your message across.

Questions and Other "Off-the-Cuff" Challenges Capturing and holding your listeners' attention is one thing, but what do you do when the tables are turned at the close of your talk—when your audience starts firing questions at you? As "Handling Q&A: The Five Kinds of Listening" reveals:

> For many speakers, the most frightening part of the presentation is the unscripted part: the question and answer session at the end. . . . What if someone asks you a question you can't answer? What if someone turns hostile? What if someone [monopolizes] the Q&A with a long disquisition on some other topic?

The key to handling Q&A is *listening* carefully to the questions and responding with the right technique. This article presents five increasingly rich techniques. The first—*giving feedback*—is the easiest: You simply provide your attitude toward or evaluation of what a listener asked. But often that isn't enough—especially with a hostile questioner. With a listener who clearly has a bone to pick with you, *paraphrase* the question in a way that gets at the person's attitude. Here's an example: "So what you're saying is that you think I'm just giving you the party line." Skillful paraphrasing will elicit a "Yes" from the questioner. He or she is now in agreement with you—and will be more receptive to your further explanation. The article provides three additional Q&A listening techniques as well as a short quiz to help you assess your listening skills.

But Q&A isn't the only time when you'll be speaking "off the cuff." As Cheryl Wiles explains in "Impromptu Speaking," you may find yourself called to pull together a presentation on the spot. "That's a tall order," she concedes. Still, you *can* snap together some strategies that will help you survive the experience—including analyzing your audience as quickly as possible before you get out there in front of them, staying focused on your message as you're talking, and addressing your comments to the entire audience rather than just to a key decision maker or a person who asks a question.

Strengthening Your Presentation

In addition to the advice offered in the first two parts of this volume, you may find it helpful to have a handful of extra tools and techniques in your arsenal for further strengthening your presentations. That's where the articles in the third and final section come in. In "Six Ways to Overcome Your Fear of Public Speaking," Mike Grenby offers additional tips for vanquishing stage fright before you give a presentation. His suggestions—which range from reciting poems to trusted colleagues while standing on a table to singing a nursery rhyme with exaggerated humor—enable you to "stretch your emotional range, which both relaxes you and makes you more charismatic." And of course, compared with surviving such appalling practice experiences, giving a mere presentation should seem easy.

In "Presentations 101," John Clayton shifts the focus to graphics. If you must use slides and other visual aids during a talk, Clayton recommends avoiding common mistakes—such as cramming too much text onto your slides, blocking the overhead screen with your body, and talking to the screen rather than your audience.

"Presentations That Appeal to All Your Listeners" and "How to Make Even Weak Speeches Great" enter a different realm entirely: building trust with your audiences by understanding and adapting to their *learning styles*. In any audience, some members will learn best by listening (auditory); others, through physical activity (kinesthetic); still others, through viewing graphics (visual). The most successful presentations appeal to all three styles—by providing evocative words, compelling pictures, and opportunities for audience members to move (perhaps by raising their hands to "vote" on something). As Nick Morgan points out, you can even use "kinesthetic speaking" to your advantage; for instance, by moving closer to your audience to emphasize a point and avoiding body language that may inadvertently send a negative message (e.g., crossing your arms communicates defensiveness).

This section concludes with "The Ten Commandments of Presentations"—practical, easy-to-follow suggestions such as "Thou shalt keep thy slides to an absolute minimum," "Though shalt know what time it is at all times," and "Thou shalt neither read nor memorize a speech word for word."

Armed with the advice in this volume's selections, you should be able to tackle that upcoming presentation with a bit less nervousness and a bit more aplomb than you expected. Remember the keys to successful presentations:

- Understanding your purpose and your audience

- Managing stage fright

- Capturing and holding listeners' attention

Your payoff for careful preparation and skillful delivery? Inspired listeners who embrace your proposal with enthusiasm—and a company that appreciates your ability to motivate others and get results.

Preparing Your Presentation

. . .

As with most challenges in life, preparation is a major key to delivering a successful presentation. The articles in this section explain how to lay the groundwork for your speech or presentation. First think about your purpose –is it to *persuade* listeners to embrace your ideas or to *motivate* them to take action, or possibly both? A clear understanding of your purpose enables you to take the next step: analyzing your audience. Who are your listeners? What do they already know about the subject matter of your presentation? How will they likely respond to your message? What do they need from you in order to heed your message?

Informed by a deep understanding of your audience's frame of mind and needs, you can move on to structuring your presentation—deciding what to say first, how to back up your ideas, and how you'll wrap up your talk for maximum impact. And to arrive fully prepared, you can take some steps to control stage fright. Your goal? To survive the first 60 seconds of your talk—when anxiety tends to be highest.

The Three Toughest Presentations

• • •

Nick Morgan

What are the toughest speeches you have to give—the ones that really give you the jitters? Is it talking frankly about a product delay to an irate user group? Telling a group of employees that layoffs are in the offing? Or analyzing some poor third-quarter numbers in front of a skeptical pack of Wall Street number-crunchers?

Those are indeed tough situations. They each involve delivering some sort of bad news, and that's not easy. But as presentations, they're not particularly difficult to construct. The key is to get the bad news out, in its entirety, right at the top. In each case, your audience will be imagining the worst, and having the bad news out where everyone can see it will immediately cut those fantasies down to size.

Speeches like these you just have to survive. But there are three categories of speeches that require more finesse: closing a big sale, launching a change effort, and persuading your board to approve a risky new investment. The key is using your listeners' energy to get them headed in the right direction.

Closing the Big Sale

To close the big sale, you must create trust. You do so by solving your listeners' problems for them, not by showing off your expertise. So begin an important sales speech with questions. You need to find out what their problems are before you can solve them.

Ideally, of course, you will have thoroughly researched the issues involved before you attempt to close the big sale. You have figured out what the problems are and how your product or service will solve those problems.

Resist the temptation to jump to the conclusion, your answer, too quickly. Audiences won't find you credible unless you spend almost as long dwelling on the problem as you do on the answer. You have to show that you not only understand but empathize with them. You're taking your audience on a journey toward the solution you're proposing, and it's essential that you begin by showing them that you know what their problems look and feel like.

If your product or solution triggers a problem that your audience doesn't know it has—if you're selling ice to the Inuit, for example—then you have to spend correspondingly longer on the problem, establishing its credibility, and yours.

> ## Close your presentation with a straightforward, polite request for action on the audience's part.

Once you've thoroughly established the problem and elicited the audience's buy-in through close questioning, then you are ready to move on to your solution. As Andrew Finlayson notes in his book *Questions That Work: How to Ask Questions That Will Help You Succeed in Any Business Situation,* "The intent is to introduce questions that show interest and the excitement that grows out of the realization that there must be a better way. If you have a positive questioning attitude about you at all times, your inquiry can create an awareness of people's character and circumstances. In turn, their answers can give direction to your actions."

Here, you have to resist the temptation to talk about the product or service itself. Rather, describe it in terms of what it can do for your audience. Take the infamous car salesperson. If he spends lots of time talking about horsepower and wheel size and "what this baby can do," he's going to bore everyone except testosterone-charged teens.

If, on the other hand, he spends some time finding out how many kids you have and begins to point out how the backseat can go down to create a bed for those long car trips to Canada you told him you take every summer—that's interesting to you. If you're one of those people who can't seem to go more than ten minutes without a drink of lime-flavored mineral water, then all those cupholders are fascinating. But the salesperson first has to notice the water bottle you're clutching and ask you about your strange compulsion to drink constantly, before he can point those cupholders out without risking your alienation.

Closing a sale requires spending some time looking at your product or service from the customer's point of view, and then telling that customer how your offer meets her needs. Successful sales pitches take imagination to prepare.

Finally, of course, you have to ask for the sale. Close your presentation with a straightforward, polite request for action on the audience's part. Make it a reasonable first step if you're uncertain about the final result—this tactic usually yields better results than asking for the moon. Get your listeners to take some small action, and they are far more likely to take the final big one you're hoping for. But don't be deceptive. It's never worth jeopardizing the relationship.

Inspiring Change

How do you kick off a big change effort? First, contrast the state of things as they are now with the state of things as they might be if the change is successful, and persuade people it's worth journeying from one to the other.

There are two ways to accomplish this difficult feat: the "burning building approach" and the "promised land picture."

The burning building approach basically describes the status quo in words so dire that only a madman or a fool would want things to continue as they are. Trust is important here, too, so don't distort the facts in order to create a false picture of terror. Those words will almost certainly come back to haunt you later when the truth emerges. Once trust with an audience is broken, it is virtually impossible to get it back.

If you've described the current situation at your company in sufficiently alarming terms, you've created a desire for change in your audience. Then you need to give that desire an outlet by *enlisting its energy in designing a solution*. The key is transforming your audience members from passive recipients into active enlistees.

This stage is where most change leadership fails. Because the leader thinks it's her job to solve all the problems the company has, she spends a lot of energy creating a solution beforehand. The result is resentment or indifference from the employees. Their thought processes run something like this: "You got me all alarmed. Now you tell me there's a way out. Why get me so worked up? You knew all along that things weren't so desperate."

Instead, you can reveal the main outlines of a plan going forward, but leave substantial parts of the picture for the audience to fill in. Then you will take the energy you've created and channel it into getting to work on the solution. That will go a long way toward ensuring that your change program will be met with enthusiastic enlistment instead of the usual suspicion, cynicism, and indifference.

If you don't allow audiences to generate energy and then release it in action, their responses will remain those of spectators. And spectators are not what you want participating in large-scale change programs with high stakes. Failure under those conditions is almost guaranteed.

The promised land picture is almost exactly the opposite of the burning building approach. You begin by describing an adequate status quo. Once again, the approach has to be honest because of the risk of the backlash when the truth comes out later.

Then, you deliver, in glowing terms, a picture of a future state that has so much allure for your listeners that they are unable to resist it. Is it an IPO that will make them all millionaires? That worked pretty well for the dot-coms until it became clear that the dream had died. Is it the opportunity to participate in historically great work? Is it the chance to become world famous, breaking all previous records for glory? Greed, glory, and fame pretty much sum up the basic human motivations in the workplace. If you're not tapping into one of those, you're probably not going deep enough.

> If you don't allow audiences to generate energy and then release it in action, their responses will remain those of spectators.

The key, once again, is understanding what your audience wants. If you misread your people and offer them an outsized prize that they're really not interested in, you'll disgust them. Or invite ridicule. The story you tell has to connect with their needs. Stephen Denning, change management expert and author of *The Springboard: How Storytelling Ignites Action in Knowledge-Era Organizations,* puts it this way: "A springboard story has an impact not so much through transferring large amounts of information, as through catalyzing understanding. It can enable listeners to visualize from a story in one context what is involved in a large-scale transformation in an analogous context. It can enable them to grasp the idea as a whole not only very simply and quickly, but also in a nonthreatening way. In effect, it invites them to see analogies from their own backgrounds, their own contexts, their own fields of expertise."

If you've held out a sufficiently alluring prize, then you've created energy in your audience once again, energy that needs outlet. At this point, you need to *enlist your audience's aid in telling you how you're going to get to that promised land.* If you do the work for the audience, all that energy gets dissipated and you won't enroll anyone in the cause. If they do the work, then your listeners will be ready to jump the hurdles and go around the roadblocks in order to get to the desired endpoint.

You can begin this work in the presentation session itself, but you don't have to complete it. It's usually better to get your listeners to work on some aspect of the path forward there in the moment, rather than the whole answer. If it all can be created by one audience on the fly, then it probably isn't that difficult to achieve, and what was all the fuss about? Rather, give out assignments for work teams going forward so that the energy continues pointed in the right direction and focused on the right problems.

Persuading the Board

Boards tend to suffer from corporate groupthink. All else being equal, they'll almost always choose the middle option, the reasonable solution, the blandest alternative. That's called exercising fiduciary responsibility. It's what boards are paid to do, essentially: keep the corporate patient alive.

So how do you get them to take radical action?

It's not easy. You can use elements of the foregoing approaches to improve your chances of success, but the needs of a board are sufficiently different from the audiences in the previous two examples that the techniques espoused there are not guaranteed to work.

Thus, you can describe a burning building or a promised land, or you can ask the board questions in an effort to determine what it is worrying about, and then speak to those worries. But none of these approaches will necessarily motivate a board to take more than incremental steps, because it has an inherently conservative role to play.

Instead, you need to *minimize the radical nature of the proposal.* Of course, honesty is essential here as in the other tough presentations. But if you frame the step you want to take as simply one more in a logical set of steps you have been taking successfully all along, you'll allow the board to fulfill its essentially conservative mission.

Robert B. Cialdini, in his classic work, *Influence: Science and Practice,* finds the most powerful leverage for this kind of change in commitment: "Once we realize that the power of consistency is formidable in directing human action, an important practical question immediately arises: How is that force engaged? What produces the *click* that activates the *whirr* of the powerful consistency tape? Social psychologists think they know the answer: commitment. If I can get you to make a commitment (that is, to take a stand, to go on record), I will have set the stage for your automatic . . . consistency with that earlier commitment. Once a stand is taken, there is a natural tendency to behave in ways that are stubbornly consistent with the stand."

Boards make commitments as a matter of routine; if you can match your desired goals with their commitments, you will find much more willingness to go along with what you are proposing.

Once again, you begin with questions. In this case, the questions should be designed to create the frame you wish to establish. How does the board see the nature of the competition? What are the threats to the markets we are currently selling in? What is the likelihood that a new competitor could come along and redefine the market away from our products?

Next, tell the board members a story that reveals the big picture of opportunity you want them to see. If the opportunity has been framed within a context of marketplace threats and change, board members will be much more likely to see that opportunity as a logical next step. Denning says that successful stories were "told from the perspective of a single protagonist who was in a predicament that was prototypical of the organization's business. The predicament of the explicit story was familiar to the particular audience. . . . The story had a degree of strangeness or incongruity for the listeners, so that it captured their attention and stimulated their imaginations. Yet at the same time, the story was plausible, even eerily familiar, almost like a premonition of what the future was going to be like."

Then, begin to describe the need that your investment will fulfill. Again, paint the picture in terms of consistency with the board's previous actions. The company has invested in factories before. Just because this one is in India doesn't mean that the issues involved are hugely different. You still have to iron out wrinkles and get the plant running smoothly. It's still all about the execution, right?

Finally, frame the investment opportunity in terms of the board's long-term vision for the company. How does this step represent a logical next step on that journey from one little factory in East Bangor to world domination? How will this step consistently and logically allow the company to get to that end state the board wants?

Don't forget to ask for the sale. And if you've enlisted the aid of a few individual members of the board beforehand, that won't hurt either. The key to succeeding in tough presentations is to use your audience members' energy to get them headed in the direction you want them to go, whether you're closing a big sale, inspiring change, or prompting a board to take action.

For Further Reading

Questions That Work: How to Ask Questions That Will Help You Succeed in Any Business Situation by Andrew Finlayson (2001, AMACOM)

The Springboard: How Storytelling Ignites Action in Knowledge-Era Organizations by Stephen Denning (2001, Butterworth-Heinemann)

Influence: Science and Practice by Robert B. Cialdini (2001, Allyn & Bacon)

Reprint C0109A

The Key to Making Better Presentations

Audience Analysis

• • •

Michael Hattersley

Presentations have become ubiquitous in corporate life and critical to careers. At some companies you wouldn't be caught dead pitching an idea or plan to more than two people without the aid of an overhead projector and a pile of acetates. Many corporations dictate strict format guidelines, while, pushing from the opposite direction, software makers offer seemingly endless iterations on products to make visuals snappier and more breathtaking. Too often, though, a presentation fails not because of image paucity, overcrowded foils, or a halting manner at the podium, but rather because of what didn't go on beforehand: a thoughtful, deliberate analysis of the audience and their likely response. What follows are seven steps to such an analysis.

1: Define your audience— or, more likely, audiences

No, not just a list of who's going to be in the room. Your audience consists of the people you want to act: the superiors whose sign-off you need, the employees who can achieve the productivity gains you outline. In almost every presentation, however, the support—or at least the neutrality—of the secondary audience will prove critical for achieving your goal. Whom do your superiors consult before making a decision? What individuals or groups have more influence over your employees' attitudes than you do?

Take the time to list every significant audience likely to have an influence on, or be affected by, your proposal. Divide them into the primary audiences, defined as the key decision makers and others whose direct support you'll need, and secondary audiences, those who will be affected by your project and who, over the long term, may have some influence on the decision makers.

2: Decide what approach is appropriate to take with this audience

Are you telling them or asking them? Most business communication falls somewhere in between. You need to take one approach when pitching a proposal to a committee of higher-ups, and another when assigning tasks to a team of your subordinates. In her *Guide to Managerial Communication,* Mary Munter offers a framework useful for thinking about which approach to take.

On the vertical dimension, plot your degree of control over the content, in two senses: how much control you have over the requisite information, and how much executive power you have to push along the matter at hand. On the horizontal dimension, chart how much involvement you need from the audience to get the outcome you're looking for. As Munter observes, "The more you control, the less you involve; the less you involve, the more you control."

Some rules of thumb for choosing the correct approach: Tell—in a polite way, of course—when you are in complete command of the necessary information and authority; for example, when you're directing a subordinate to carry out a routine task. Sell when you're in command of the information, but your audience retains the ultimate decision-making power. Consult when you're trying to build a consensus toward a particular course of action; for instance, when you need to persuade colleagues to back your proposal to top management. And join when your point of view is only one of many; say, when you're serving as your unit's representative to an interdepartmental strategy session.

In general, you're telling down and joining up. But not always: Enlightened you will often need to solicit the ideas of subordinates (consulting) or lobby superiors for a favorable decision (selling).

3: Anticipate how they are likely to respond

If you've defined your audiences with enough granularity, the likely answer: mixed. It's not uncommon to find one audience segment supportive, a second neutral, and a third, hostile.

Audiences that already support you—those in the positive camp—need to be given a plan of action and motivated. Let them know how important they are, and what they can do to support you. Neutral audiences are most susceptible to rational persuasion; share with them the sequence of events and analyses that convinced you this was a good idea. Hostile audiences probably won't ever actively support you, but by showing that you understand their point of view and explaining why you still believe in the project, you may move them to a position of neutrality.

When doing the analysis at this stage, pay careful attention to the motives of individuals and groups. Some people may support you because they're your friends; don't let this lure you into a false sense of security about the attitudes of your wider audience. Some members of the audience may oppose your idea on the merits. Dealing with them, you'll be best served by delivering your message frankly, in the process acknowledging their concerns and the arguments they make.

A few may oppose you simply because they can't stand the prospect of your success—a boss who may fear being outshone, colleagues who are your rivals or who simply don't like you. This is the hardest kind of opposition to overcome because the people who embody it are unlikely to admit the real grounds for their response, and may develop some very creative reasons for rejecting your plan. Two possible strategies for handling them: First, give them a way out, perhaps by incorporating their suggestions, sharing credit, or supporting them toward a corollary success. Second, gain the support of those in authority over them.

4: Determine how much they already know

Nothing is more boring to audiences than a rehash of overly familiar information, and nothing more frustrating than trying to decipher a presentation pitched way over their heads. What's the minimum amount of information that you need to summarize to lay the foundation for your argument? What additional information do they need to understand and judge your proposal?

5: Ask yourself if your proposal is in their interest

Obviously related to (3), this cuts to the heart of audience analysis. Successful managers put themselves in the shoes of the people who will be listening: If you were them, what would motivate you to offer your support? How, precisely, will they benefit? Generic possibilities include more money or prestige, saving time, solidifying a friendship, gaining authority, avoiding conflict or embarrassment, improving status, having one's job made easier, and being on the winning side.

In the worst cases, there will be no apparent benefit; the message looks like unmitigated bad news. This is your invitation to drill down: Why is this announcement or proposal going to hurt my audiences? Having answered this, you can at least show that you understand, and sympathize with, their point of view. Look for ways to soften the blow. Can you make the case that your strategy is the best of a bad lot, that the alternatives are worse? Is it possible to hold out hope that things may improve in the future?

6: Sell benefits, not features

Too many managers believe that the sheer force of logic will convince others to support what they propose. Big mistake. The tools of rational persuasion will only work if they convince your audiences that the action you wish them to take will serve either their interests or a greater good.

This means selling benefits—what the audience will gain—rather than features, however fascinating, important, or elegant those features may seem to you. For example, customers may be supremely uninterested in the underlying technology of a new MIS system, the intricacies of which you find fascinating and know in detail. But they're likely to be quite interested in the savings in time and money that such a system can bring to their operation.

7: Make sure you've tailored the structure of your presentation to your audience

A manager thoroughly convinced of the wisdom of his or her proposal usually feels an understandable pressure to tell all. Don't try. An audience can only absorb a few key points in a presentation. Make sure you've picked the ones you want it to remember, and that these stand out.

High-school speech teachers are fond of saying, "Tell them what you're going to tell them, tell them, and then tell them what you've told them." Up to a point, this is good advice. By the end of your first few sentences, your audience should understand exactly what you're proposing. Only if it knows where you're going, will it be able to follow you. Then, as you progress, signal clearly how each key point fits into your overall argument.

The body of an effective presentation accomplishes two key goals: It sells the benefits of your proposal and neutralizes opposition. The order in which you pursue those goals depends on the attitude of your audiences. If they are generally hostile, you need to confront their objections immediately. Your most powerful arguments will have no effect if you haven't won their undistracted attention. Until a hostile audience knows you understand and, to some extent, share its concerns, it'll be hard to move.

If your audience's objections are subtle—"Maybe there's a better solution"—or liable to arise later, after it's had a chance to reflect or talk with others, address those objections only after you've explained the merits of your own case. Often the best way to disarm opposition is to present alternative positions as reasonable, but slightly less preferable than your own proposal. This conveys your objectivity and maturity of judgment, while enabling you to point out the downside of the alternatives. Such an approach is particularly appropriate when your audience holds a wide range of attitudes toward your subject; whether it agrees with you or not, everyone feels included in the discussion.

An adequate conclusion tells the audience what you told them. An excellent conclusion looks to the future by emphasizing the benefits to the audience of adopting your position. It also outlines next steps, demonstrating that you not only know where to go, but have a plan for getting there. Make sure, too, that you clearly signal that you're concluding. Audiences will usually pay a lot of attention to your beginning, less to the middle, and a lot to the end. Letting them know you're almost finished gives you the opportunity to drive your main point home when attention is at its highest.

For Further Reading

Guide to Managerial Communications by Mary Munter (1992, Prentice Hall)

Management Communication: Principles and Practice by Michael Hattersley and Linda McJannet (1996, McGraw Hill)

Reprint U9610B

Build a Presentation That Motivates

• • •

Nick Morgan

Earnings last quarter hurtled downward. You think you know how to turn the slide around in Q2, but it's going to require getting everyone to work a little harder this quarter as well as a little smarter. You've got the smart idea. Now you just need to persuade your employees to work a little harder.

But that's no easy task when everyone is already working 24/7/365, or pretty close to it. How can you motivate them to give a little more? You're facing them tomorrow at 0900 hours. What are you going to say?

The answer is you're going to structure your speech so that it follows a universal human pattern: decision making. You're smart enough to know that just telling them isn't good enough. Unless your employees own the decision, they won't act on it.

Decision making follows five clear steps. Your presentation needs to lead your audience through those five steps. Your audience needs to go on the decision-making journey with you. Each step has to happen at the right time.

> Structure your speech so that it follows a universal human pattern: decision making.

The first step in decision making is to realize that there is a problem. Without that realization, there is no need for the audience to commit to a change. So get your audience's attention by telling a brief story that illustrates the problem. What will your story be? That depends on your particular situation. You might relate a conversation you had with a disappointed Wall Street analyst who was thinking about downgrading your stock. That will work well if your employees have some equity in the company. Otherwise they'll just be thinking about the 1,000,000 options you have.

Second, you'll dive into a thorough and honest analysis of the situation. That exercise corresponds to the fact-gathering that people undertake when they know they have a problem. What are the causes of the downturn? What are all the ins and outs of your supply chain? What does your customer satisfaction data look like? The key here is not to pull any verbal punches. Tell it to 'em straight. Don't point fingers. But don't avoid painful truths.

Next, you'll get to the good part: your solution. If it's going to be controversial, lay out three alternatives and tell, in order, why each one won't work. Then, describe your favored solution—and describe its pitfalls, too. The point is to walk them through the decision-making process, after all, so if there are other obvious alternatives, and pitfalls to your own, don't avoid them. If you do, the audience will start creating them at the water cooler after the talk, and all your hard work will be for nothing.

Fourth, you'll spell out the benefits of the choice that you want them to take. The key issue here is to help them to visualize the good things ahead of them on the road you want them to take. If you dwell on the negatives at this point, you'll simply inspire them to gloom, not action. So don't threaten. Rather, help them over the difficult hurdle of actually making a decision by painting alluring pictures of possible (but real) happiness that awaits them.

Finally, you need to get them started on the action that you want them to take. So give them a small, easy step to take right there, in the room. You'll find that it makes the follow-up steps seem much more possible.

Once people have made a decision and take a modest step toward realizing the benefits of that decision, they've done the hardest work. The rest may take all of the second quarter and involve a lot of long hours, but it's relatively easy by comparison.

What might that small step look like? It could be creating a to do list for each department or group. It could be filling out a diagnostic exercise that shows where departmental opportunities for growth exist. It could take the form of a commitment to a series of steps to be taken later. If it involves that sort of abstract commitment, make sure that you have the audience do something physical, such as write down their individual goals on an index card.

Once you've completed the action step, avoid the temptation to summarize. The old rule of "tell 'em what you're going to say, say it, and tell 'em what you've said" is guaranteed to bore an audience every time. It was very popular in the U.S. Army, where superior officers could lock up soldiers who didn't do what they were told. Businesspeople don't have that luxury today—so avoid demotivating your audience through boredom, or coercion.

You can order people to act, but the harder you push, the more push-back you'll get. Rather, the smart leader takes her employees down the decision-making path, letting them do all the hard work of commitment themselves. If you do it right, you'll have a team of people who can't wait to get to work turning those numbers around.

Reprint C0107D

How to Structure a Persuasive Speech

• • •

The greatest short speech ever given is Lincoln's Gettysburg Address. In just slightly more than 250 words—roughly two minutes' talking at normal speed—Lincoln put the Civil War and the battle of Gettysburg in the context of the nation's constitutional history and proposed that the best way to honor those who had fallen in that terrible fight would be to finish the work of preserving the union in a "new birth of freedom."

It's a masterpiece of restrained pathos. But it has another lesson to teach us as well: it's brilliantly organized for maximum persuasive effect. What organizational secrets did Lincoln use to give his speech its rhetorical power? Can speakers today use his tricks to give their own speeches clarity, brevity, and punch? Herewith is Lincoln's model, followed by three variations to use when the circumstances of the speech dictate an alternate approach.

Describe a Situation

Lincoln begins with the situation at hand. The civil war, the battle of Gettysburg, and the dedication ceremony are all mentioned in crisp, clear phrases. But note that Lincoln actually starts his speech with an apparent look backward. "Four score and seven years ago our fathers brought forth on this continent a new nation, conceived in liberty and dedicated to the proposition that all men are created equal."

Why start here? Precisely because Lincoln wishes to frame his eulogy in the context of the constitutional history of the country. He's telling us what is at stake—our personal freedoms, and the life of the country. The story that Lincoln is telling doesn't begin with the battlefield, but rather back at the creation of the United States itself. In this fashion, he raises the ante of the day well beyond the battle—as grim as that was—and sets the lives of the soldiers who perished against the continuation of the country.

The lesson for anyone designing a presentation today is to be clear about the story that you wish to tell. Begin at the beginning of that story. But you can do that only if you know exactly what you want the audience to get out of the speech. You must frame or define the situation precisely with the end in mind.

Give the Audience a Problem

Next, Lincoln pulls the rhetorical rug out from under his audience by telling them: "But, in a larger sense, we cannot dedicate—we cannot consecrate—we cannot hallow—this ground." He adds a complication to his description of the current situation. He creates a problem. Why can't we dedicate this ground? After all, that was the ostensible point of the occasion. Thus, he propels his story forward by making the audience wonder how indeed they can accomplish the consecration they're all expecting.

This is the key step in a persuasive speech. It's the moment at which you either take your listeners with you or lose them for good. Lincoln succeeded because his rhetorical move was unexpected—it was exactly opposite to the bromides about honoring the dead the audience might have reasonably anticipated. The best problem statements accomplish this reversal by taking your listeners somewhere they weren't quite expecting to go. The tactic not only makes your speech more interesting, it also suggests that you're worth listening to because you have insight into the situation that no one else has.

Offer a Solution and
Suggest an Action

Instead of merely grieving at the battlefield, Lincoln suggests, we would better honor the dead by finishing the work they began. "It is for us the living, rather, to be dedicated here to the unfinished work which they who fought here have thus far so nobly advanced." In other words, let's get on with winning the war and putting the country back together.

> The lesson for anyone designing a presentation today is to be clear about the story that you wish to tell.

This solution points the assembled listeners toward the action Lincoln desires them to take. "That we here highly resolve that these dead shall not have died in vain—that this nation, under God, shall have a new birth of freedom—and that government of the people, by the people, for the people, shall not perish from the earth." It is a rhetorical action ("we resolve"), but an action nonetheless, to maintain this experiment in democracy on earth. All good speeches close with an action for the audience—either actual or rhetorical. The action may be small, but it should be significant.

Lincoln's insight was to take this "problem-solution" structure and apply it to a eulogy, something generally considered to be an ornamental speech more suited to flowery phrases than tight logic. He made his case brilliantly; he persuaded his audience to offer up the deaths of the soldiers of Gettysburg on the altar of the living Republic. But could he have organized the speech in other ways as well? What other organizational formats are possible for presentations?

Present a Decision to Be Made

Had Lincoln wanted to present a series of options for the audience to choose among, he would have proceeded a little differently. First, he would have begun by defining the problem: "We cannot dedicate—we cannot consecrate—we cannot hallow—this ground." Then he would have developed a list of criteria for evaluating a series of possible solutions to this problem. Next, he would have listed all the relevant solutions and evaluated them against his criteria. He would pick the best solution and suggest ways to implement it, discussing the various issues that might arise during implementation. Lincoln, of course, wanted to give his listeners one option only, precisely because he was so afraid they might choose others.

This format—definition, criteria, solutions, evaluation, selection, implementation—is effective for helping or guiding an audience to choose among options. Rhetorically, you should present the option you intend the audience to favor at the end of your list, because audiences tend to remember best things they hear last.

Deliver Bad News

If Lincoln had considered his task to be one of delivering bad news—the terrible toll of death on the battlefield— he would have begun by describing briefly the background to the immediate situation that gave rise to the bad news. It's the usual way that eulogies are begun. This device gives the audience time to prepare for the blow. Foreshadowing helps, but you don't want to make them wait too long. The audience will resent bad news delivered in the middle or end of a long speech, because it seems deceptive. So give the bad news immediately after you ready the ground. Then, you may present various options for the audience to take in responding to the news, and follow the decision-making structure for the rest of the presentation. Or, you can use the following structure, one useful for imparting information.

Impart Information

Had Lincoln intended only to present important information to his audience, he would have followed a general presentation model that works particularly well when time is limited and you want to make sure you've covered all the rhetorical bases. First, outline the situation. Then, describe your specific role in it. Next, tell what action you took and what the results were. Finally, offer your analysis or recommendations for the path forward. This format is useful for updating your boss—or the board—on a work in progress. This structure works well when you have the situation well in hand and you don't really want to re-open the decision-making process. Lincoln needed a persuasive structure because he had to unite an uncertain populace behind him.

These four structures—problem/solution, decision making, bad news delivery, and information imparting—cover virtually every presentation one could possibly make. When you next have to give an important speech, take the time to analyze your situation and your audience, and pick the structure that best suits the occasion. You'll then be in a position to give a successful presentation. It may not rise to the level of the Gettysburg Address, but at least you'll be thinking like Lincoln.

Reprint C0005B

Coping with Stage Fright

How to Turn Terror into Dynamic Speaking

• • •

John Daly and Isa Engleberg

You're about to make an important presentation. People are streaming into the room. Your boss is sitting up front. Important clients are sitting in the second row. Your boss stands to introduce you and you walk toward the stage.

As you approach the front of the room your confidence wanes. Your stomach starts doing somersaults, your palms are sweating, and your mouth feels parched. You pick up your notes and your hands are shaking. Thank goodness, you say to yourself, for the lectern. As you start to speak you hear your voice quiver and you feel your skin beginning to blush.

Welcome to the world of stage fright!

You are not alone if you have had this experience. Almost everyone has. Even people who regularly appear in front of large audiences experience stage fright. The great American actress Helen Hayes was known for throwing up in her dressing room before every single performance during a career of more than 50 years. Luckily, researchers in communication and psychology have identified several strategies that can help you overcome your nervousness.

Preparation Is Critical

Know Your Audience and Setting

Successful speakers know it is critical to acquaint themselves with both the audience and the setting before making a presentation. Talk to a few people who will be in the audience. Ask who else will be attending and what interests them. Find out what audience members know about the topic. Discover ways this audience is similar to, and different from, other groups you have addressed.

Just as important, look over the setting before your presentation. Find out where you will be speaking and get there early. Check the room's acoustics, sit in a chair and see the room from the audience's perspective. Test all the equipment. Assume nothing.

Prepare Your Material

Never underestimate how important good preparation is to reducing your anxiety. When you know what you want to accomplish, what you are going to say, and how you are going to say it, you will be less anxious. Mark Twain claimed it took him three weeks to prepare an "impromptu" speech. Another great speaker, Winston Churchill, said it took him six to eight hours to prepare a 45-minute presentation. Here are four rules for preparing your presentation.

1: Know your topic. Audiences can sense when you are bluffing, and when they feel you are unsure of your material, they lose confidence in you. Being unprepared also makes you, the speaker, anxious. You have concerns about unanswerable questions; you worry you don't have enough to say; you fear you are wrong about something. Avoid these anxiety-producing thoughts by being the expert.

2: Prepare more material than you think you will use. If you have to give a five-minute presentation, develop enough material for 15 minutes. It's better to pare down than to run out of things to say.

3: Imagine questions people might ask. Come up with answers before you give your speech. Either incorporate the answers into your presentation or hold them in readiness in case those questions are asked. Savvy corporate leaders and public officials use this technique when planning to meet the press. A day or two before the press conference, leaders are briefed by staff about likely questions and possible answers. That review makes them more confident. They feel better prepared.

4: Memorize the first minute of your presentation. You experience your greatest anxiety at the beginning of a speech. Having the start of your presentation memorized makes you more comfortable. You also may want to memorize the last minute of your presentation in order to conclude with conviction.

Focus on Your Audience, Not on Yourself

Most of us do not like to feel conspicuous. When you talk to a group of 20 people, there are 40 eyes staring at you. If you start thinking about all this attention, you may begin to focus on how you look and sound rather than on communicating your message to your listeners. Your attention shifts from your audience to yourself. When you become self-focused, your stage fright increases and the quality of your performance suffers.

Television broadcasters know this. In studios they avoid looking at monitors while the camera is on them. If they watch themselves, they'll be distracted. Some public-speaking books suggest that you practice in front of a mirror. Bad advice! Try it and you will see why. When you start talking, you'll notice your facial expressions, your hair, and your gestures. And, you'll think little about your presentation.

What should you do when you feel self-conscious during a presentation? Talk to individual listeners. Pick out a person. Tell yourself that you are going to talk right at him until he begins to smile. Smile and you'll find that he'll probably smile back. Then, move to another audience member and think, "I'm going to talk directly to this person until she nods her head." As you talk, start nodding your head and watch as she reciprocates. What you are doing is shifting your attention away from yourself and onto the audience.

Relabel Your Physical Symptoms Positively

Much like an athlete getting ready for a big game, your body gets "up" when you make a speech: your heart beats faster, your palms get sweaty, your legs seem a little wobbly. When experiencing these feelings, some people think, "I'm scared." Other people say to themselves, "I'm excited." Physiologically, there is little difference between fear and excitement. The real difference lies in what you call it.

Think of something adventurous you do—riding a roller coaster, scuba diving, a bicycle race. What are your feelings at the start? Many of these physiological reactions are no different from the ones you have when you start a presentation. The difference is that you call these activities fun while labeling presentations scary. Same physiology, different labels. So next time you start a speech, label the experience positively.

Labeling is only the first step. People who have a great deal of stage fright often talk themselves into being nervous: "This is going to be awful . . . Why am I up here? . . . I'm going to make a fool of myself . . . People are going to walk out . . . What if they hate me?" When you talk this way, you may begin to believe it. Experienced speakers convince themselves that they'll do a great job: "I'm going to be effective . . . This is exciting . . . What an opportunity . . . I know my stuff and I am going to convince this audience."

Use the energy you experience—don't be used by it. Before your presentation, walk around if you can, take some deep breaths, stretch. When you start your presentation, move, use gestures. Let your nervous energy animate your speech.

Avoid Rigid Rules

People with stage fright often have very rigid rules about what makes a good presentation. One computer executive who often experienced stage fright told us that "every good speech starts with a joke." An anxious scien-

20 Strategies for Reducing Stage Fright

1. Understand that your listeners want you to do well.
2. Believe you know more than your audience.
3. Familiarize yourself with the setting.
4. Get to know some members of the audience before you speak.
5. Choose topics you know something about.
6. Prepare your message; indeed, overprepare.
7. Imagine questions that might be asked.
8. Memorize the first and last minutes of your presentation.
9. Focus on your audience, not on yourself.
10. Don't practice in front of a mirror.
11. Never tell the audience you are nervous.
12. Label your physiological excitement as positive rather than negative.
13. Talk positively about your presentation to yourself.
14. Turn your energy into something positive.
15. Get rid of your "rigid" rules about speaking.
16. Be flexible and adaptive during your presentation.
17. Understand that no presentation is "that important."
18. Remember that you are not a good judge of how nervous you appear.
19. Believe compliments on your presentation.
20. Think! Plan ahead to avoid problems.

tist believed that "all speeches should have three main points." A VP related that "every presentation must include color graphics." These speakers dearly loved their rules about speaking. Consequently, they were haunted by them. In truth, none of them are mandatory rules of good speaking. Is it possible to give an excellent presentation without any jokes? Sure. Do all excellent presentations have three major points? Of course not. And many outstanding briefings have no graphics at all.

Here's something else to think about: Most people are more comfortable answering questions in Q&A sessions than they are giving speeches. You'd think it would be the opposite. Presentations are prepared in advance. But it is difficult to prepare for every question: you think "on your feet" when answering questions. Sounds as though questions should be more nerve-wracking. But not so for most speakers. Why? Because people have far fewer rigid rules about question-answer sessions. On the other hand, almost everyone has strong rules about speeches. Be flexible. Drop the rigid rules!

Think Before You Speak

Learn some simple ways to manage your anxiety. Think before you make a presentation so you can avoid or control what makes you nervous. For example, what if your hands shake when you speak? Place your hands on the lectern. Or suppose the notes you hold rattle as you speak? Why not put your notes on a clipboard? If you are so nervous that the clipboard shakes, lay the notes on a table or lectern. What if you blush when nervous? The blushing starts at your chest and slowly works up your neck. Why not wear a scarf or turtleneck that hides the blushing?

You Don't Look That Nervous

Has this happened to you? You finish a presentation and people come up and congratulate you. While you thank them for the compliments, you're thinking, "They're just being nice. They really think I did a lousy job. They could see I was shaking and sweating." Research tells us you're probably wrong: speakers are often inaccurate in their assessments of how nervous they appear. But these inaccurate perceptions feed stage fright. When you think you look anxious, you feel more apprehensive. And the cycle continues until it detrimentally affects your performance.

Reducing stage fright is not easy. It requires conscientious work on your part. You'll have to try the techniques we've described in front of real audiences. But, if you are well prepared and willing to discard your misconceptions about speaking, you can reduce and maybe even conquer your stage fright. And you will gain the flexibility and confidence to transform a fearful ordeal into an invigorating and successful experience.

For Further Reading

Avoiding Communication: Shyness, Reticence, and Communication Apprehension edited by John A. Daly, James C. McCroskey, Joe Ayres, and Timothy Hopf (1997, Hampton Press)

Conquer Your Speechfright: Learn How to Overcome the Nervousness of Public Speaking by Karen Kangas Dwyer (1998, Harcourt Brace College Publishers)

Overcoming Your Fear of Public Speaking: A Proven Method by Michael T. Motley (1997, Houghton Mifflin)

Never Be Nervous Again by Dorothy Sarnoff with Gaylen Moore (1987, Fawcett Columbine)

Reprint C9906A

Delivering Your Presentation

• • •

You've carefully prepared your presentation—your purpose is clear, you understand your audience, you structured your speech, and took steps to control your stage fright. The selections in this section explain what you can do *during* your address to further boost your chances of getting the results you desire. By analyzing examples of famous successful speeches, you can learn how to grab your listeners' attention from the outset— and then hold it during the rest of your talk. Some keys? Engaging your audience actively in the topic of your presentation and using your physical presence to keep listeners focused on you.

This section also addresses what many people see as the most frightening part of giving a presentation: the question-and-answer section that comes at the end of your speech. To be sure, Q&A and other forms of impromptu speaking can unnerve even practiced presenters. But by sharpening your listening skills, you can adapt your response to each questioner in ways that defuse tension and open audience members' minds to further points you have to offer.

Are Your Presentations Inspiring?

One of the Great Speeches of History Offers Some Surprising Lessons

* * *

Has one of your speeches ever caused your listeners to riot in the streets for three days? That was the result of President John F. Kennedy's June 26, 1963 address to the citizens of West Berlin. More than a million people lined the Rudolf Wilde Platz in the divided city to hear the young American president who had been so severely tested on his resistance to Communism by the Bay of Pigs fiasco, the Cuban Missile Crisis, and the Berlin Wall itself. It may well have been the largest gathering of its kind in human history. The West Berliners' need for reassurance was great; they felt isolated by the newly built wall.

Within a few minutes, speaking through an interpreter, Kennedy created a delirium of enthusiasm in his listeners, prompting them to demonstrate for three days until the police and military were able to reestablish control.

What was the secret of Kennedy's power? How did he connect so strongly with his audience? What are the lessons of this short, simple, and yet extraordinary speech? Can they be applied to the typical business presentation?

Looking at Kennedy's speech in some detail yields six lessons that can help make your presentations, if not riot inducing, at least more memorable than the average business talk.

1: Write It Yourself

Kennedy wrote the short speech himself and insisted on delivering it over the objections of the military command. The generals worried that the speech would cause the nervous citizens of Berlin to riot—as, in fact, they did. But the point is that Kennedy avoided the bureaucratic and lengthy in his talk partly because he didn't have the time to create anything wordier. He wrote the speech in haste over the few days prior to the event, on his way to Berlin. Lacking the usual governmental resources to help him, he was forced to keep it simple.

The speech also reflected his beliefs more closely than a speech penned by his speechwriters ever could have. And that's the first lesson for business speakers. Rather than having your staff prepare some notes for what they think you should say, take the time to figure out the main points for yourself. Then get your researchers to fill in any missing detail. That way the presentation is more likely to reflect your beliefs and thinking.

2: Keep It Simple and True

This speech belongs to a select group of memorable speeches that clock in at 10 minutes or less and stick to one clear theme. It is the coincidence of integrity, brevity, and simplicity with an important occasion that makes for golden rhetoric. Many presentations are long-winded and simpleminded; few manage to say the right thing at the right time in the fewest possible words. Lincoln's Gettysburg Address, Martin Luther King, Jr.'s "I have a dream" speech, and even the Sermon on the Mount all combine these ingredients unforgettably. Reagan's elegy on the subject of the Challenger disaster comes close; time will be the judge of that speech's staying power. In each case, the absolute clarity and conviction of the speaker came first. Then came the simplicity of delivery. Finally, the success of the speech in the moment ensured that history would remember it forever.

In Kennedy's case, the speech is about freedom and the unity of all free peoples, including the citizens of

Berlin. The enemy of freedom is Communism, says Kennedy, but it cannot prevail against free peoples everywhere. That's it. "Freedom has many difficulties, and democracy is not perfect, but we have never had to put up a wall to keep our people in," says Kennedy. The words are unforgettable because they confront directly the hard reality facing Berliners. He doesn't try to palliate the ugly truth of the situation. He meets the seriousness of the political crisis with matching passion and strength.

3: Meet the Needs of the Audience

Perhaps most fundamentally, Kennedy understood the needs of the citizens of Berlin and addressed them. They had just been shut off from freedom by the Berlin Wall and were understandably feeling isolated and in danger of being abandoned by the West. Would America stand by them?

Kennedy brilliantly addressed those concerns by talking about freedom being indivisible: "So let me ask you, as I close, to lift your eyes beyond the dangers of today, to the hopes of tomorrow, beyond the freedom merely of this city of Berlin, or your country of Germany, to the advance of freedom everywhere, beyond the wall to the day of peace with justice, beyond yourselves and ourselves to all mankind.

"Freedom is indivisible, and when one man is enslaved, all are not free. When all are free, then we can look forward to that day when this city will be joined as one and this country and this great continent of Europe in a peaceful and hopeful globe. When that day finally comes, as it will, the people of West Berlin can take sober satisfaction in the fact that they were in the front lines for almost two decades.

> Many presentations are long-winded and simpleminded; few manage to say the right thing at the right time in the fewest possible words.

"All free men, wherever they may live, are citizens of Berlin, and, therefore, as a free man, I take pride in the words *Ich bin ein Berliner*."

By making common cause with them around the issue of freedom, Kennedy met the most deep-seated fears of the audience with reassurance. "Ich bin ein Berliner" was exactly what the city wanted to hear.

4: Appeal to Something Larger than Self-Interest

We humans are at once noble and selfish. If you appeal solely to our self-interest, we will listen, and perhaps appreciate your words. But we won't respect you. We know what pandering is, and we are quick to recognize it. The tendency to pander is what makes most political speeches today so forgettable. Kennedy understood that a principle was at stake, one that might be difficult and dangerous to uphold for the citizens of Berlin (and the free world) but one that was worth the fight. To really get your audience on its feet—and rioting—you have to show them how self-interest and larger principles coincide, such that personal sacrifice is worth it if it becomes necessary.

5: Identify with Your Audience

You can't preach to an audience about grand things, however, if the audience perceives you as aloof from them. It's another paradox that gives speakers trouble. You need to find the ways in which you and the audience are alike and make those clear early on. Your listeners will then be willing to open themselves to your message. It's a way of building trust early on. Audiences want their speakers to have credibility, and they want to be able to trust them. You can't create the latter unless you find a way to connect with your audience.

Kennedy accomplishes his identification with the Berliners with the famous phrase, which he utters in the first minute of his speech: "Two thousand years ago the proudest boast was *Civis Romanus sum*. Today, in the world of freedom, the proudest boast is *Ich bin ein Berliner.*" Of course, the president goes on to cement the identification with his brief sermon on freedom, but the initial move comes early, before the important themes of the talk have been established. Thus, Kennedy realizes that the first step he has to take is one toward his audience, in the essential figurative sense that shows that he understands their problems.

6: Repeat a Memorable Phrase

Even in this short speech there is a good deal of repetition. It is the single most important linguistic device of speechmaking. Audiences have difficulty remembering what they hear—all the studies show that listeners retain only a small percentage of the presentations they witness—and repetition helps them keep up and gives them a sense of mastery of the occasion. So resist the temptation to try to be clever at your audience's expense. Instead, look for ways to repeat your basic message memorably. Kennedy uses the "Ich bin ein Berliner" line twice, at the beginning and at the end of the speech. He repeats another key phrase as well:

"There are many people in the world who really don't understand, or say they don't, what is the great issue between the free world and the Communist world. Let them come to Berlin. There are some who say that Communism is the wave of the future. Let them come to

The Jelly Doughnut Speech?

It's impossible to discuss Kennedy's Berlin speech without at least a passing reference to the slight slipup that prompts some to call this speech the "jelly doughnut speech." In addition to describing a resident of Berlin, the German word "berliner" also refers to a type of German pastry. The translation of Kennedy's impassioned statement, "I take pride in the words *Ich bin ein Berliner*," can be literally taken to mean "I take pride in the words *I am a jelly doughnut*." (To say "I am a Berliner," Kennedy should have said, "*Ich bin Berliner*.") Fortunately for Kennedy, the tolerance for error is higher in public speech—it's a looser genre than, say, the written word. Accuracy is indeed important, but truthfulness and passion are more so.

Berlin. And there are some who say in Europe and elsewhere we can work with the Communists. Let them come to Berlin. And there are even a few who say that it is true that Communism is an evil system, but it permits us to make economic progress. *Lass' sie nach Berlin kommen*. Let them come to Berlin."

It's rare that the historical moment, the cause, and the speaker come together to produce unforgettable speechmaking, but when they do, the words can echo down the years to inspire us when the moment, the cause, and the speaker are gone. And we can take the lessons of the historical moment and apply them to our own speeches. Great rhetoric may be the result. Even if your listeners don't finally riot in the streets.

For Further Reading

Lend Me Your Ears: Great Speeches in History revised edition (1997, Norton)

The Lost Art of the Great Speech: How to Write One—How to Deliver It (1999, AMACOM)

Reprint C0101A

Five Winning
Ways to Begin a
Presentation

• • •

The number of people who can reliably begin a presentation with a joke that works is very small—and most of them host their own talk shows. Why do so many speakers still attempt the near impossible? Why do they put themselves under such unnecessary pressure? The first couple of minutes in a presentation are nearly always the worst—why tempt the fates with an approach virtually guaranteed to fail?

Try this at home. Watch Jay Leno give his opening monologue on a typical night. Count the number of jokes. Count the number that fall flat—even with the wildly pumped-up studio audience. Then ask yourself how many times you laughed. The ratio will be something like 20–10–2. The last number may be slightly higher if it's Friday night, and you're glad you've made it through another week.

The point is that good jokes are hard to find, harder still to deliver, and quick to expire. Don't do it. Don't tell opening jokes. Just say no to "one-liner" humor at the beginning of a presentation.

There is a better way. There is even some emerging research from the fields of neuroscience and cognition indicating that the better way may be grounded in our brain structure.

Let's begin by rephrasing the question that gets speakers into trouble in the first place. Too many speakers ask themselves, "How can I get this dull talk started with something that will show my audience I'm really a fun person?"

Instead, the question you should ask yourself is, "How can I best draw this particular audience into the subject I'm there to talk about?"

And the answer to that question is, tell a story. Well-told stories engage us from the start because they have narrative drive—we want to find out what happens. Even if we've heard the story before, the recognition itself can bring pleasure, especially if there's a new twist to the tale. And if the story has a point, we can apply it to our current situations even if we've been told the story many times before.

But the need for stories may be even more basic than this. In his book *The Literary Mind*, Mark Turner, a member of the Institute for Advanced Study in Princeton, N.J., argues that our minds work fundamentally by taking both old and new stories and projecting them on our current situations to enable us to make sense of them. Turner's work links with others in the field of cognition to illuminate the ways in which we learn new material.

Specifically, he says, the narrative form that best fits this activity is the parable. Take, for example, the story of the ox and the donkey. Once upon a time there was a wealthy farmer who could understand the language of animals. His ox would work all day, and come home each night, exhausted and grumpy, to the stall he shared with the donkey. The ox noted that the donkey was always well rested and fed, because the farmer never seemed to work him very hard.

Unlike the ox.

One day, the ox could stand it no longer. "How is it that I work my hooves to the hocks every day and you just get to lie there doing nothing? It's not fair!"

And the donkey replied, "Try this. Tomorrow, when you're taken out to the field, pretend to be sick. Lie down and refuse to get up, even if they beat you. Try this for a day or two, and you won't have to work hard again."

Unfortunately for the two animals, the farmer chanced to be listening to this conversation. Thus, when the ox seemed to get sick the very next day, the farmer told his workers, "Go get that lazy donkey and make him do the ox's work!"

A parable like this can be used in a number of ways in a business context. For example, you could use it when recognizing an unsung division. Just pick your "donkey" group with care, or leave it unspecified.

According to Turner, many of our significant mental activities follow from what we do with parables like these.

> " . . . good jokes are hard to find, harder still to deliver, and quick to expire."

First, we're always looking to predict the consequences of our actions and the actions and events around us. Good stories like this parable help us do that because we can take the results of the story and imagine how they would work out—in parallel situations—for ourselves.

We also evaluate events and their consequences—would we like what happened to the donkey to happen to us? Further, we plan and explain our own actions and those of others using the mental schema provided by countless stories like this one. To put it another way, we're constantly playing out scripts in our minds that feature the same kinds of actors, actions, and attitudes that stories give us.

How does this mental map apply to the beginnings of presentations? If this is the way the mind works, speakers can best warm audiences to their messages by casting them in story form.

Here are five ways to take advantage of the inner workings of your audience's mind. These are sure bets, when done correctly, for engaging your audience from the start and ensuring that it will stay with you to the end.

1. Tell a parable. In order to tell an engaging parable, you need to know two things. First, what is the underlying emotion you are trying to evoke in your audience? Second, what is the key decision point or dilemma you want your audience to consider? You can then choose a parable that will relate well to both topic and audience.

To pick a simple example, let's say you are running a start-up company, and some of the workers are losing hope because it's year two and there's no sign of profitability on the horizon. You want to rally the troops. You need to persuade them to hang in there for the long haul, and to endure the trying conditions of 140-hour workweeks and lousy pizza for another year at least. The underlying emotion, then, is frustration, and the decision point is whether to give up the pursuit or not. An appropriate parable, then, is one like the tortoise and the hare from *Aesop's Fables*.

If the only parable you can come up with seems too trite to engage your audience, dress it up by customizing it for your particular group. So it becomes the AARP tortoise and the HMO hare, for example. You can liven it up further with some key details that relate to the current situation that will amuse and interest your listeners. The point is that the audience will enjoy the old tale re-told with fresh details.

In addition to *Aesop's Fables,* folk tales from a variety of traditions are good sources of parables. Religious traditions, depending on the audience, can be another good source. And there are a host of modern parables in collections specifically selected by subject matter and type of audience.

2. Tell a personal anecdote about how you got engaged in the particular topic. It can even be funny. The more prestigious the speaker is for particular audiences, the more charming they will find this opening gambit. A CEO can tell his employees about how he was playing video games with his kids one night when the phone rang. He picked up the phone, and it was Jane, the senior vice president, on the line. "Why are you calling me on a Friday night?" the CEO asked. "I'm in the middle of a video game." "Well," responded the SVP, "Then I've got good news and bad news. The good news is that the new product launch is wildly successful. The bad news is that you just lost your video game."

That was a joke. If you didn't laugh, we've proven our point about how difficult humor is to do well. If you did laugh, your day just got a little better. Personal anecdotes work well provided the detail is relevant and the

Memorable Beginnings: How a Few Great Speakers Started Their Presentations

Art Buchwald Speaks to Law Graduates

On May 7, 1977, Buchwald delivered the commencement day address at Catholic University's Columbus School of Law, in Washington, D.C. After a few words of thanks, Buchwald began his speech as follows:

> I am no stranger to the bar. I first became interested in the law when I was working in Paris for the *Herald Tribune,* and I covered a trial which had to do with a couple caught in a very compromising situation in a Volkswagen. Now, everyone in France was interested in the case because it had to do with such a small car. The defense lawyer argued that it was impossible to do what the couple had been accused of doing in a Volkswagen. The judge said he didn't know if this was true or not, so he appointed a commission to study it. It took them six months to render their verdict, and they said, "It was possible but very difficult."

Salman Rushdie Addresses Columbia University's Graduate School of Journalism

On December 11, 1991, author Rushdie came out of hiding long enough to address the assembled dignitaries at a dinner honoring the two-hundredth anniversary of the First Amendment. Note how Rushdie uses his parable as a way to create sympathy for his plight, threatened as he was by the Ayatollah Khomeini's death sentence for blasphemy.

A hot-air balloon drifts slowly over a bottomless chasm, carrying several passengers. A leak develops; the balloon starts losing height. The pit, a dark yawn, comes closer. Good grief! The wounded balloon can bear just one passenger to safety; the many must be sacrificed to save the one! But who should live, who should die? And who could make such a choice?

In point of fact, debating societies everywhere regularly make such choices without qualms, for of course what I've described is the given situation of that evergreen favorite, the balloon debate, in which, as the speakers argue over the relative merits and demerits of the well-known figures they have placed in disaster's mouth, the assembled company blithely accepts the faintly unpleasant idea that a human being's right to life is increased or diminished by his or her virtues or vices—that we may be born equal but thereafter our lives weigh differently in the scales.

It's only make-believe, after all. And while it may not be very nice, it does reflect how people actually think.

I have now spent over a thousand days in just such a balloon; but, alas, this isn't a game.

Winston Churchill Speaks to Parliament

On May 13, 1940, Winston Churchill addressed Parliament as the new prime minister, responsible for a country that was late in readying itself to defend against the Nazi menace. Note how he puts his listeners right in the middle of the situation; his eloquence grows ultimately out of the simple, straightforward narrative with which he begins:

> On Friday evening last I received from His Majesty the mission to form a new administration.
>
> It was the evident will of Parliament and the nation that this should be conceived on the broadest possible basis and that it should include all parties.
>
> I have already completed the most important part of this task. A war cabinet has been formed of five members, representing, with the Labour, Opposition, and Liberals, the unity of the nation.
>
> It was necessary that this should be done in one single day on account of the extreme urgency and rigor of events.
>
> . . . I now invite the House by a resolution to record its approval of the steps taken and declare its confidence in the new government.
>
> . . . I say to the House as I said to ministers who have joined this government, I have nothing to offer

point of the story doesn't get lost in the trivia. Since people are rarely as interested in the minutiae of your own life as you are, err on the side of caution.

3. Ask a question that either surfaces the underlying emotion you wish to evoke or begins the overall story

but blood, toil, tears, and sweat. We have before us an ordeal of the most grievous kind. We have before us many, many months of struggle and suffering.

You ask, what is our policy? I say it is to wage war by land, sea, and air. War with all our might and with all the strength God has given us, and to wage war against a monstrous tyranny never surpassed in the dark and lamentable catalogue of human crime. That is our policy.

You ask, what is our aim? I can answer in one word. It is victory. Victory at all costs—victory in spite of all terrors—victory, however long and hard the road may be, for without victory there is no survival.

Let that be realized. No survival for the British Empire, no survival for all that the British Empire has stood for, no survival for the urge, the impulse of the ages, that mankind shall move forward toward his goal.

I take up my task in buoyancy and hope. I feel sure that our cause will not be suffered to fail among men.

I feel entitled at this juncture, at this time, to claim the aid of all and to say, "Come then, let us go forward together with our united strength."

that you wish to tell. The classic example of this is the campaign question presidential candidate Ronald Reagan asked his audiences again and again when he was running against President Carter: "Are you better off than you were four years ago?" That question accomplished both tasks; it brought up the frustration voters were feeling after several years of "stagflation," and it allowed Reagan to begin the story he wished to tell, about the bright future he was going to bring America if elected.

4. Tell a bit of a story from a classic movie or a popular TV show. Film is the medium that affects the widest possible audience in our culture today. TV runs a close second. Both are filled with parables that relate to current situations. So why not borrow their power and appeal? You need to tell enough of the story so that anyone who hasn't seen the movie or the show can figure out what you're talking about, but not so much that you give away an ending, or lose your listeners in the trivia. Once again, the point is that your short story has to relate organically to the subject of your talk.

5. Play a scenario game that contains the elements of your broader story. This one is for experienced presenters only, but it can be the most energizing for the listeners because it gets them to do something active. A game is a form of participatory parable with fixed rules governing the beginning, middle, and end. So, for example, if you're giving a talk about the ubiquity of the Internet, set up several computers in the room and offer a prize to the first person or team that can find a particular bit of information using the Internet.

Each of these opening gambits uses elements of storytelling and parable that respect the way your audience's minds work and uses that knowledge to engage the audience in compelling and entertaining ways.

For Further Reading

Aesop's Fables illustrated by Charles Santore (1997, Random House)

Bright Air, Brilliant Fire: On the Matter of the Mind by Gerald M. Edelman (1993, Basic Books)

Descartes' Error: Emotion, Reason, and the Human Brain by Antonio Damasio (1995, Avon Books)

How to Write and Give a Good Speech: A Practical Guide for Executives, PR People, Managers, Fund-Raisers, Politicians, Educators, and Anyone Who Has to Make Every Word Count by Joan Detz (1992, St. Martin's Press)

Lend Me Your Ears: Great Speeches in History edited by William Safire (1997, W.W. Norton)

The Literary Mind by Mark Turner (1996, Oxford University Press)

The Presentations Kit: 10 Steps for Selling Your Ideas by Claudyne Wilder (1994, John Wiley & Sons)

Searching for Memory: The Brain, the Mind, and the Past by Daniel L. Schacter (1997, HarperCollins)

Reprint C9812A

Six Ways to Grab Your Audience Right from the Start

• • •

Beverly Ballaro

Hares and tortoises aside, slow and steady does not always win the race; this truth I discovered literally the hard way. A lightning roundhouse kick to the ribs, launched a millisecond after the referee's bark of "*Hajime!* (Begin!)," had left me flattened, breathless, and endowed with fresh insights into the importance of seizing the initiative and thus control of a situation.

Modern karate, the records tell us, was founded by an Okinawan gentleman, Funakoshi, who stood an unassuming five feet tall and whose sensibilities were so courtly, he could not bear, well into the 20th century, ever to utter the word for *socks,* considering such a reference beneath his dignity.

Yet Funakoshi had a deep understanding of what fate awaited his warrior ancestors who failed to grasp the first opening in a contest: "Then, quick as a flash, with one stroke it was over" (Vince Morris, *Zanshin*, 1992).

> ## The debunking of a common myth can ease the introduction to a difficult topic.

While the stakes are mercifully different for the average public speaker or writer today, the wisdom of the samurai swordsmen's fast and dramatic approach will still pay dividends to all writers who keep it in mind: To grab—and keep—your audience's attention, it is critical to make a powerful connection at the very outset.

If you fail to hook your readers or listeners with your first few sentences, it won't matter how brilliant the rest of your business plan or analysis or speech might be because nobody is going to be paying much atten- tion. Conversely, if you succeed in engaging your audience at the very beginning, you will increase their receptivity to the whole of what you are trying to communicate. Here are six quick and easy formulas to hit the ground running.

1: Make It Personal

There is no faster way to tune readers or listeners into your message than to package that message in the form of a story. Personal accounts—whether they focus on adversity, nostalgia, or triumph—can establish an instant rapport with your audience.

One of the more gripping openings I have ever wit- nessed was authored by a man at the peak of his career. Confounding the audience's expectation of a dry analy- sis heavy on statistics, he began his assessment of the evolution of his profession with a compelling descrip- tion of his own inner-city origins:

> We ended up moving to . . . a typical tenement—
> rats, roaches, sirens, gangs, murders. Our heroes were
> the drug dealers because they gave candy to the kids.

On another occasion, I listened to a forensics expert deliver some fairly dense remarks on DNA testing to a mixed audience consisting both of colleagues who "spoke his language" as well as laypeople, most of whom (myself included) wouldn't recognize an electron microscope if one hit them over the head.

But it didn't matter. The expert began with an anecdote about how grateful he had been to be flying home to the United States from a country where he had been engaged in the sad and gruesome task of using the latest genetic technology to identify civilian war casualties buried in mass graves:

> As I reflected on the human tragedies I had witnessed . . . the deep blue Adriatic swelled below [my plane]. The local time was 2:30 P.M.—that's 8:30 A.M. Eastern time in the United States. The date was September 11, 2001.

The audience let out a collective gasp and stayed riveted through the scientific explanations that followed.

2: Throw Out a Quirky Fact

The revelation of an offbeat statistic or the debunking of a common myth can ease the introduction to a difficult topic or even woo skeptics.

For example, an author who is pitching his trend-bucking proposal for a streamlined, rather than gourmet, cookbook to a publisher points out that, according to a recent survey, the average American currently spends 15 minutes preparing dinner.

An artist writing a background of how he got into the business of crafting funeral urns, starts his spiel with the following sentence:

> When the average adult is cremated, the volume of ashes is about three quarts, or enough to fill a shoebox.

With this memorable fact, he engaged his readers' attention for an analysis of some of the more technical aspects of his craft.

3: Put Them on the Edge of Their Seats

If you manage to pique your readers' curiosity in the beginning, chances are they'll stick around for the answer to the question you raised.

The head of an institution writes a progress report and maps out challenges that lie ahead. He begins his appeal with a quiz, asking his audience to ponder the related significance of the years 1866, 1953, and 2040:

> In 1953 Crick and Watson first described the double helix of DNA. Any guesses about 1866? Does anybody recognize Gregor Mendel, who published his milestone paper on inheritance in peas that year? If the next big milestone happens according to this pace, that discovery will occur in 2040.

The Most Attention-Grabbing Speech Opening Ever

Most businesspeople still think that you should open a speech with a joke. Bad idea—you're nervous, and the audience is trying to decide whether to listen to you or not. Unless you're Robin Williams, a joke is a hard thing to get across perfectly. Don't do it. Instead, break the rules.

Tactfully, of course. Elizabeth Dole pulled off what is probably the highest-stakes, most attention-grabbing opener ever during the Republican National Convention of 1996, by breaking one time-honored rule that no one expected her to break: She left the podium.

Impossible you say—what about the microphones, the teleprompters, the television? How could she leave the podium? She had a wireless mike, she had memorized the speech, and the cameramen had been briefed about where she was going.

Plus, she told the audience what she was doing as she did it. And even more important, she made a connection between her surprising move and the rest of the speech. She said she was leaving the podium to come down into the audience to tell them "about the man I love."

Her point was that she felt so strongly that she had to break out of the normal restrictions to make her point.

It was theatrical, but it worked. The audience went crazy for Dole—*Elizabeth* Dole. In fact, talk of her presidential campaign began that night. Last year, she was elected to the U.S. Senate.

By creating suspense as to what lies ahead, the author invites his audience's participation and anticipation at the same time.

4: Draw a Hypothetical Scenario

This approach can focus on either the past or the future and provide either a positive or negative contrast.

A company that manufactures "smart" technology tries to create excitement in potential investors or consumers with a positive angle:

> Imagine a world in which a building senses earthquake vibrations and adjusts the resistance of its walls to withstand the tremors. Self-navigating cars travel the nation's highways, slowing down, changing lanes, and "choosing" the fastest route, as appropriate. These might sound like ideas straight out of a Star Trek script, but they will become realities sooner than most people think.

A Web site designed to raise awareness of the issues related to deafness establishes empathy between the target audience and the cause it promotes through negative imaging:

> Imagine a world without sound. A remote, silent landscape void of normal conversation and music. . . . Imagine not being able to hear the birds singing

early in the morning or a favorite song on the radio. For an estimated 28 million Americans afflicted with hearing loss, this silence can be overwhelming.

5: Create a Series of Vignettes

To draw your readers into the big-picture point you are trying to get across to them, it can be helpful to orient them with a series of connected "reality snapshots" written in the dramatic present tense:

In New York City, a doctor notifies the health department after seeing two cases of encephalitis with unusual features.

In Washington, D.C., an emergency room physician's suspicions are raised after a patient suffering from mild, flu-like symptoms reveals that he is a postal worker in a facility near the nation's capital.

In New Jersey, a pediatrician takes a hard look at what appears to be a spider bite on a child's arm, after learning that the infant had recently been brought to her mother's New York news office.

Vignettes such as the three above can then be linked together with an opening punch line–like sentence:

Thanks to the efforts of alert clinicians, Americans have quickly come to understand that we are living in a new era in which the symptoms of common threats—encephalitis, the flu, or spider bites—are mimicked, as in the New York, Washington, and New Jersey cases, by lethal, unexpected foes such as the West Nile virus or anthrax.

6: Use a Pertinent Quote

Although quotations generally do not make for as compelling openings as statements offered in the author's own voice, they can, particularly if they manage to invoke irony or humor, set the stage effectively for what is to follow.

A document presenting an innovative communications product, for example, can rely on quotes that illustrate the historical evolution of that industry:

This telephone has too many shortcomings to be seriously considered as a means of communication. The device is inherently of no value to us.

—*Western Union internal memo, 1876*

Who the hell wants to hear actors talk?

—*H.M. Warner, Warner Brothers, 1927*

There is no reason anyone would want a computer in their home.

— *Ken Olson, president, chairman and founder of Digital Equipment Corp., 1977*

The author thus quickly puts into perspective for his readers the benefits of risk taking and the importance of entrepreneurial vision.

Regardless of which approach you choose, the bottom line remains the same: Don't cast your line without first baiting your hook.

Reprint C0306E

Are You Listening to Me?

Here's How to Get Your Audience to Tune in

• • •

Richard Bierck

As Shakespeare's Falstaff noted 500 years ago, "It is the disease of not listening, the malady of not marking, that I am troubled withal." Falstaff was deliberately avoiding duties he considered unpleasant. Today, we have those who are deliberately tuned out, and those who are simply overloaded. But neither group will hear you. How do you tell who's attentive and who isn't? And how do you get the latter group's attention?

"People give a lot of nonverbal messages about whether they're listening," says Doe Lang, a New York City psychologist who specializes in communication and image. "As a rule, if they're crossing their legs, fidgeting, or looking around a lot, chances are you don't have their rapt attention." (Lang concedes that this may not apply around the globe—in Japan, for example, direct eye contact is generally viewed as overly confrontational.)

Methods to Lure Your Audience Back

Once identified, the wandering mind can be lured back into the presentation or conversation by using a variety of techniques. Here are some ways to rein in the aurally absent while making presentations to large groups.

Change What You're Doing

A sudden pause or change in vocal tone can have the same effect on a preoccupied mind that turning off a television set has on a sleeping viewer: They both awaken. Of course, speakers who use this technique successfully tend to create another hurdle: They must follow the pause with something particularly clever or insightful, lest they be accused of loopy histrionics. So if you use this one, have something ready.

Ask a Question

When you suspect an audience member of taking a mental vacation from the presentation or conversation, ask her a piercing question related to one of your points. If she indeed wasn't listening, she will be now. "Often, I'll turn my next thought into a question," says G. Richard Shell, a professor at the University of Pennsylvania's Wharton School, whose speaking skills are reflected in numerous teaching awards. "I'll ask some of the restless to help me out. But I'll give them a chance to hear it. I'll say, 'So I'm going to ask you a question . . .' and everybody perks up."

Get the Audience Involved as a Group

For example, ask for a show of hands on a practice or opinion, however tangential it may be to the topic at hand. Doing so will rouse the laggards, and you can use the "votes" as springboards to further discussions and questions.

Identify an Attentive Member of the Audience

The trick is to develop a nonverbal rapport with him or her. When you "catch" someone not listening and then recoup his attention, make him the new person you are relating to. Perhaps other nonlisteners will come along. In smaller groups, such as departmental meetings with fewer than 10 participants, there's far more room for give and take, and less chance of losing someone when you take the floor. But it happens nonetheless, often because they are preoccupied with their work or what they are about to say.

Give Your Audience a Listening Test

"If I think there may be some listening problems," says Mark Gordon of Vantage Partners, a Boston-based consulting firm that specializes in negotiations, "I may say: 'Let me go on for a couple minutes, and then I'm going to ask you some questions.' This not only gets them to listen, it also prepares them for questions about what I've said, so they don't feel that I'm springing a trick question."

Quickly Introduce the Business at Hand and Ask for Input

If audience members are involved initially, chances are they will stay involved after they're no longer participating verbally. But getting people involved can lead to interactions that can stir up tensions, causing them to stop listening. "People who are strongly averse to interpersonal conflict stop listening when things get tense," says Shell. "Suddenly, they need to go to the restroom or to their next appointment. If this happens, the speaker must manage the dynamics. One way to do this is to change the focus to something outside the room. The goal is to get people off the emotional level and back on task."

Tailor Your Language to the Listening Styles of Your Audience

Let's say you're speaking to a person who frequently looks to the left. Barring the possibility that there is

Reading Your Audience's Body Language

Successful speakers have enough presence of mind that they can monitor their audience's body language during the course of a presentation and react accordingly. The result is a dynamic presentation that treats the audience with respect, pausing when it needs to pause, moving on when it needs to move on.

Most of us read body language unconsciously. When someone is fidgeting and not making eye contact, we sense that we're not enthralling that person. When an audience member greets our proposals with a frown, crossed arms, and a shake of the head, we get it—that person is not buying what we're offering.

But it's useful to develop your skills in reading body language consciously, both because you can become more precise in your abilities to understand the reactions of various sections of the audience, for example, and because you can sense a change in the audience's opinion more quickly than if you leave the work to your subconscious.

You can analyze your audience's responses using three continua that, taken together, sum up the various possible responses to your presentations.

Open—Closed

Signs of openness may include nodding, smiling, and other attentive, positive facial gestures. A seated audience will usually orient itself in your direction if it is open to you. Signs of closed behavior may include turning away from you, averted eyes, crossed arms, muttered (negative) comments to neighbors, frowning, and shaking the head. Open behavior on your part will increase the likelihood of open audience behavior—but how much your audience likes your message also matters!

Engaged—Disengaged

When an audience collectively disengages, it is a powerful response that few speakers ultimately fail to pick up. Squirming increases, eye contact becomes minimal, and everyone's shoulders slump down and away from the speaker. The key word is "ultimately," however; early, subtler signs of disengagement are important to respond to because at that stage the audience can be won back. Look for changes in the faces in front of you; try nodding to selected members of the audience to see if they nod back. Approach one or two people in different parts of the audience; if they don't connect with you readily and eagerly, it's time for a change of pace. Try asking the audience a few questions or give them something new to do.

Allied—Opposed

Allied audience members will unconsciously mimic your behavior; opposed audience members will do the opposite. Build on the allied behavior by approaching those audience members and having brief exchanges with them. You can either ignore those who are opposed (if they are few in number) or tackle them head on by engaging them in prolonged Socratic dialogue. This last tack is not for the inexperienced or nervous; fainthearted speakers had better stick to their texts and not chance ad-libbing with the opposition.

—Nick Morgan

something interesting to look at, this is the type of behavior that psychologists attribute to people who characteristically visualize while listening. "This behavior is cross-lateral. The side of the face that they're using tends to indicate the side of the brain that they're using," says Lang. "When they're looking left, they're actually accessing the right hemisphere of the brain—the imaging side." To hold their attention, you'll need language rich in concrete metaphor so that they may "see" analogies. Instead of "eliminate the disparity," try "bridge the gap." Instead of "characterized by errors," try "brimming with mistakes."

If a person in your audience frequently looks up, he or she may relate more to feeling and touching than to images. For these listeners, forgo "discernible" for "palpable," use "texture" instead of "nature," and generally give them verbal images they can hold on to.

If your listener frequently looks to the right, he or she is accessing the left side of the brain: logic, deduction, reason. These listeners want things to add up, so make sure they do. Moreover, they won't start daydreaming when you haul out your kit bag of analysis. These are skilled listeners who are literally oriented and can follow your words as though they were on a page. But they have one thing in common with the most intermittent listeners: They are allergic to boredom. So try to keep things interesting. The best way to do this in large group settings is to use humor—preferably of the self-deprecating variety. This assures your listeners that you aren't trying to intimidate them. And, says Gordon, "it keeps them listening for the next time it happens. Intermittent reinforcement is a huge driver of behavior."

Typically, humor is not as effective in small group settings. "You don't want to be grim in meetings," says Shell. "You can make a joke to bring people back, for instance. But in a small group setting, speakers command attention by their seriousness of purpose, presence, or their attention to some goal that people can pick up on. It could be the seriousness of wanting to finish on time."

Yet, a speaker's tone and pace should vary with the nature of the audience as a group. Though individual attention spans vary, one's station in life plays a part in determining whether one's mind is in the room or elsewhere. Generally speaking, the more important a person is, the more mental distractions there are to lure his attention away from the speaker. "It all comes down to the opportunity costs of being there," says Shell. "CEOs have enormous risk in terms of opportunity costs—whether they should be there or somewhere else. The speaker carries that burden."

For those who haven't mastered their material, this burden becomes unbearable. Speakers must be extremely conversant with their material so they have the wherewithal to deal with the nuances exhibited by fidgety audiences. "It's like a lawyer making a summation to the jury—you have to get your case across," says Shell. "To be effective, it's a given that you know your material cold."

The ability to sense what's going on in the minds of your audience members and make changes on the fly is what separates the great speakers from merely good or effective ones. If you're focused solely on delivering your presentation just as you had rehearsed it, you won't be sensitive to what's going on in the room and you'll stand no chance of corralling the inattentive. So be prepared to speak extemporaneously. Reading the nonverbal behavior of the audience will let you know when to improvise. Only by being extraordinarily well-prepared can you pull it off. Curing the disease of not listening begins with the speaker.

Reprint C0104A

You Are the Best Visual

Use Your Own Physical Presence to
Drive Home Your Presentation's Point

* * *

Judith Humphrey

John F. Kennedy's inaugural address. Martin Luther
King, Jr.'s "I Have a Dream" speech. Prime Minister
Margaret Thatcher's Falkland Islands address. All great
speeches. Each has earned a place in history. What do
they have in common? None of these speakers were
using visual aids. Just imagine John F. Kennedy standing before the world at his inauguration with a
flipchart that read, "The Torch Has Been Passed." Or
Martin Luther King showing a slide with a clip art
image of a black girl and a white girl holding hands.

Such props clearly have no place in these stirring speeches. In fact, they would detract from the drama of the moment. Why?

Great leaders understand that they are the best visual. They instinctively know that their message will come through best if the audience looks at them and listens to them—with no distractions. Audiences that divide their attention will only be able to partially commit to you.

Let's look at the logic behind this statement. The goal of any business presentation, speech, or conversation should be to lead others. Of course, there are many possible secondary goals of a presentation—to entertain, to inform, to share expertise, or to persuade. *But if you are speaking as a leader, your only goal should be persuading the audience to think or act differently.*

The best way to create a persuasive leadership moment is to become the audience's focal point. If you are committed and engaged, the audience can see it in your face, in your gestures, in the way you walk, in the way you stand, in the way you hold your head high. Your body becomes the very best visual for portraying your leadership message.

We say a great leader has "presence." That is, the speaker is *present* in a way that engages everyone in the room. Many great speakers realize that being present gives them power to persuade. So they do everything they can to maximize their visibility.

President Woodrow Wilson broke with a 113-year tradition by personally reading his messages to Congress, rather than sending them to be read by a clerk. His reason? He wanted to show "that the President of the United States is a person, not a mere department of the Government hailing Congress from some isolated island of jealous power, sending messages, not speaking naturally and with his own voice." Of course, Wilson lived in an era before the temptations of PowerPoint slides and multimedia presentations. But the truth still holds.

> Audiences that divide their attention will only be able to partially commit to you.

Motivational leaders today also realize the importance of presence. Tom Peters is admired for his charisma, in part because he makes the most of his physical presence. He often moves away from the podium when speaking, moving back only to look at his text. But a wide variety of personal styles are possible for the committed, passionate speaker. For example, creativity guru Edward De Bono uses his physical presence in a very special way. He creates his presentations on the spot, while sitting in front of his audience.

Props that enlarge your presence can be useful. For example, family members flanking a politician are a "prop" that says the politician has family values. The leader who delivers an address from a battlefield, as Abraham Lincoln did at Gettysburg, clearly shows a concern for those who fell in the struggle. These props don't have the distancing effect of words on a slide.

Emphasis on your physical presence should not detract from the importance of your message. In fact, physical presence must underscore your message. By concentrating on you visually, the audience can actually hear your message better. That's because an audience "hears" with its eyes.

Winston Churchill well understood that if you could visually distract an audience, the speaker would have less power. During Parliamentary debates, he would smoke his cigar while his opponents were speaking. First he would insert a hat pin through his cigar. As the ash grew longer, people in the audience sat staring at the cigar, wondering when the ash was going to fall off. Because they were focused on his cigar, they would stop listening to his Parliamentary opponent.

Churchill realized that in a battle between the "eye" and the "ear," the eyes have it. No speaker, no matter how effective a presenter, can control the room when the audience is visually distracted.

Managers often use PowerPoint or other visual aids, believing that their audience can absorb more of their talk if they listen *and* look. But that's not the case. When speakers use visuals, they create competition for the audience's attention between the eye and the ear. And because the eye is a much more powerful sensory device than the ear, the eye wins. Your information gets star billing; your leadership qualities finish a distant second.

PowerPoint slides are usually a dumbed-down version of the narrative script you are delivering. Visuals rely on bullet points; you speak in full sentences, with illustrations and stories. Slides are dispassionate; your voice and gestures provide passion and emphasis. So in deflecting the audience's attention away from you to the bullet points, you're reducing the quality of your material and its impact on the audience.

But it gets worse. Visual blight overwhelms many slides. Far from underscoring your points, these "visually challenged" slides frequently illustrate mental confusion. Lou Gerstner, when he first joined IBM, complained: "I have never seen foils [overhead transparencies] like in this company. There must be a manual that says every foil must have four circles, two squares, two triangles, 16 arrows, and as many of them as possible should be three dimensional—with shading—and at least four colors." How many business presentations have you sat through where just puzzling out the cluttered information on the screen caused you to lose several minutes of the speaker's talk?

Speakers love these slide shows because they function as a "crutch" or security blanket. It's easier to show prepared slides—particularly if they've been blessed by the PR department or your technical people, or your boss—than to speak from your own passion.

Some speakers defer to visuals because they are nervous. The darkened room appeals to them. They become narrators. But the ugly truth is that the leader can't lead from the sidelines using a crib sheet. Two examples:

- Speakers often delegate speech creation to a subject matter specialist, who loads up each visual with elaborate graphics and excessive content. The result is that the bells and whistles take center stage, relegating the presenter and his or her message to a supporting role. The opportunity for leadership is lost in a sea of information. Michael Dell, Chairman and CEO of Dell Computer, succumbed to this approach in a recent presentation. His people had put together a glossy visual presentation, but as Dell spoke he paid little attention to what was on the slides. In fact, at several points the statistics he was reciting bore no relationship to the numbers that were on the slides.

- At a glitzy presentation given by the CIO of a Fortune 1000 company, state-of-the-art slides dazzled the audience. After the presentation, a member of the audience came up to him and said, "Do you have a card—the card of the firm that produced the presentation?" Ouch. But the audience member was simply giving credit where it was due.

In sum, if you want to achieve your maximum power, focus the audience's attention on yourself. Only then will you have control of the room. Only then will you experience your full potential to reach and motivate an audience. Only then will you be a convincing leader.

Reprint C0110E

Handling Q&A

The Five Kinds of Listening

• • •

For many speakers, the most frightening part of the presentation is the unscripted part: the question and answer session at the end. While some thrive on the improvisatory challenge, others fear the nightmare possibilities. What if someone asks you a question you can't answer? What if someone turns hostile? What if someone wipes out the memory of all your hard work by monopolizing the Q&A with a long disquisition on some other topic?

We'll give you specific suggestions for each of those situations, but first let's consider the reason you gave the speech in the first place. Most likely, you were asked to speak to a particular audience. You wrestled with the topic, did your homework, calmed your nerves as best you could, and set off to find the podium. So far, it's all been about you. But as soon as you arrive in the room to face the crowd, something changes. The speech is no longer about you. It's about them. Once the speech starts, you need your listeners more than they need you. Without them, it's just a rehearsal.

Fast forward to the end of the talk. It's time for Q&A. Now, you'll find out how well you did. Did you in fact communicate?

The only way to know is to listen. Handling Q&A successfully depends on good listening. Good listening is a skill that can be developed, and one that is poorly understood by most speakers.

There are five levels of listening: feedback, paraphrasing, clarification, empathy, and active listening. Most of us are adept only at the first level. Developing your skills at the other levels will greatly increase the comfort and ease with which you handle question-and-answer time.

Giving Feedback

Feedback is fundamentally a reaction. The other person says something, and you say something back, giving your attitude toward or evaluation of what was said.

You're a senior manager, and you are responsible for developing a new software product that is late to market and way over budget. You've been asked to rally the troops and give them some hope, a way forward, assurance that the proverbial light at the end of the betaversion tunnel isn't the Microsoft train. You finish your talk with some stirring words about pioneers and landing on the moon that you hope didn't sound too goofy under the circumstances, and it's time for Q&A. The first question comes from a quiet looking guy in the back.

"Forgive my skepticism, but why should we believe you when we've been hearing similar stuff from senior management for months now, when what we really need is more help, more support, and a whole heck of a lot less red tape?"

It's the question you most feared. You begin to think that you made no progress whatever with these people. All your work was for nothing. You take a deep breath, and respond.

"Like I said, we're committed to getting you more people. We're frankly struggling to hire as many people as we need. We can use your help—tell your friends. As for the rest of it, we just don't have more money to throw at the project now. And we'd like to think we've gotten as much of the bureaucracy out of the way as we can. After all, we set you up in a separate building to get away from the stuff that goes on around here. Next question?"

It's a response. On the surface, it's an unexceptionable one. After all, it responds to each of the points raised by the questioner. And yet, it will do little to deal with the attitude the questioner has, and he's probably not alone. Could you have done more?

Paraphrasing the Question

At the second level of listening, you paraphrase the question, mirroring questioner's points. Let's look at how that works in the example.

> "So what you're saying is you think that I'm just giving the party line, when what you really need is more help and less bureaucracy, is that right?"

See what happens? The questioner's likely response is "yes." From the start, you have him agreeing with you. You can then go on to give your feedback, as above, but at least you have created a more receptive listener, because you've got him nodding at your paraphrase of his question. But there are even better ways to respond.

Clarifying the Issues

The third level of listening involves working a little harder with the questioner's words to identify his real concerns. Let's see how that would work here.

> "So what I hear you saying is that you've got two main problems you want help on: not enough

Are you a Good Listener?

Good listening involves seeing as well as hearing. Non-verbal communications often can tip you off about the real issues involved in workplace dialogue. Here are four quick tests of how the nonverbal "conversation" is going.

Always remember that "body language" is multi-determined; crossed arms can mean defensiveness or simply that the person is chilly. You must always know the person and the context to evaluate nonverbal communication.

Is the body language open or closed? Are the arms unfolded or crossed? Is the person with whom you're talking turned toward you or away from you? Are the hands visible? These are signs of degrees of openness.

Is the body language engaged or disengaged? People who are engaged in discussions tend to find ways to move closer to one another. The opposite movement can mean disengagement.

Is the body language allied or opposed? People who are allied in opinion or loyalty tend to adopt the same body position in conversation. Look for the person who moves at the same time you do, ending up in a similar position.

Is the body language committed or uncommitted? The sum of the other three adds up to commitment. If you see signs of openness, engagement, and allied behavior, you may be ready to close the deal. Evidence to the contrary indicates reservations, and it may be a good idea to try to explore the areas of resistance in order to deal with them verbally.

people, and too much bureaucracy. The first is probably the most important. Is that right?"

Once again, you've established a level of agreement with the questioner. By clarifying, however, you've gone one step further. You've shown the audience that you can think on your feet and that you're trying to sort out the vital issues as you go. You keep better control of the Q&A session in this way. Moreover, if you get agreement, you've actually helped the audience do its thinking. It's hard to remember information presented orally. Audiences appreciate it when longer points are accurately summarized.

Empathetic Listening

The fourth level, listening with empathy, means showing that you understand the feelings of the questioner. The empathetic listener finds similar emotions within his or her own experience and shares them with the questioner. Let's see how that would work in this example.

"You know, I've been there, too. Don't forget I worked in a start-up in '92, one that was strapped for people and drowning in red tape too. I know what you're going through."

Empathy has the inestimable advantage over the first three levels of listening in that it shows the other person that you understand his situation. Even if you can't offer much help, at least you've aligned yourself with the questioner. That in itself can go a long way to defusing hostile questions and reassuring nervous audience members.

The danger with empathy is that your own expression of solidarity can overwhelm the questioner's words. He may end up feeling upstaged. Take care that your empathetic response doesn't last longer than the question that triggered it, or your answer may sound insincere. The fifth and final level of listening avoids this trap.

Active Listening

With active listening, you identify the underlying emotions in the questioner's words. This is potentially the most powerful listening response, because it is usually emotion behind the phrases that prompted the question in the first place. When you respond to the real reason that the questioner spoke up, you get to the heart of the issue—even if you never provide any concrete answer. Let's see what the active listener would say in our example.

> "It sounds like you feel really alone out there, without much support. You're frustrated because you're putting in all this hard work, and all you feel you get back from us is red tape. Is that it?"

Here, if you've listened accurately, you're likely to get a truly heartfelt "yes!" from the questioner, and often from other members of the audience. By accurately identifying the emotional state of the questioner, you've validated the aspects of his mental state that are most important to him. You've not only aligned yourself with the questioner, but you've also allowed true healing to begin. By labeling emotions that are not usually acknowledged, you've brought them out into the open air and created the conditions for them to be dealt with positively. Active listening incorporates empathy, but goes beyond it. You don't have to use such attention with every question, but it is almost always helpful.

What do you do if someone asks a question you can't answer? Be honest in your response. Tell the questioner you don't know the answer, but you'd be happy to find out. Or turn the question back to the audience, asking for their input.

What do you do if someone turns hostile? Use active listening to acknowledge the anger. Find out the reasons for it. Acknowledge the valid ones and reject the ones that are not accurate. Then, politely and firmly, move on.

How do you prevent someone from monopolizing the Q&A period? If the question looks like it will go on longer than a minute, interrupt politely with "excuse me, but we're almost out of time, and out of concern for other members of the audience who have questions, let me stop you there and answer as best I can." Or, "Since we're almost out of time, I'd be happy to take your question off-line to give it the time it needs."

The best answers come from good listening. Successful handling of Q&A begins with a speaker who realizes that a presentation belongs to its audience.

Reprint C9902C

Impromptu Speaking

The Secret Is to Prepare for Spontaneity

• • •

Cheryl Wiles

In the movie *The Hunt for Red October,* Jack Ryan (played by Alec Baldwin) is summoned to the Pentagon by his boss for a briefing to the Joint Chiefs of Staff on recent Soviet submarine activity. As the two of them sign in to the high-level briefing, Baldwin whispers, "Who is giving the briefing?" His boss calmly says, "You are." The imposing doors swing open and Baldwin is confronted with the expectant faces of the Joint Chiefs.

While most of us won't be called on to address such an august body in the midst of a national crisis, we can relate to the panic that registers on Baldwin's face at that moment. Impromptu speaking isn't easy, and this truth hits home whenever we are asked to put something together on the spot. We want to be clear and direct, interesting and informative, persuasive and concise. That's a tall order, especially when we are nervous.

A lot can go wrong when speaking spontaneously before an audience. How will you remember everything you want to say? What if a pontificator undermines the logical flow of your sales pitch? How will you deal with trick questions that are meant to embarrass you, or worse, lead you to make a mistake? Fortunately, with a little advance work, even the most terrified impromptu speaker can improve.

Here's the secret to successful, impromptu speaking: preparation. While "impromptu" may seem to convey "winging" it, the best speakers avoid that trap. Don't confuse impromptu speaking with casual, off-the-cuff remarks. In today's business environment, there's no such thing as passively attending a meeting—you need to be prepared at all times to explain your objectives and make the case for your decisions. Impromptu speaking is about packaging information that you've already thought through. This is good news, because most of us do not feel confident winging it. Remember the last impressive "impromptu" talk you admired so much? Chances are, it was rehearsed, in some form or another, prior to the delivery. The moment felt fresh and sponta-neous, but the message was crystallized at an earlier time.

So begin your impromptu speech preparation by first deciding how, when, and why you are most likely to deliver your next talk. For example, will it be at a staff meeting? If so, then anticipate the topics your manager is likely to bring up during the meeting.

Next, think about the key points you'd like to make. Who will be at the meeting? What will persuade the attendees to champion your initiatives? Once you anticipate the objections and questions that may come up, turn on a video camera and deliver a brief "impromptu" speech as if it were the real thing. Ask a friend or your spouse to ask you some tough questions on tape. By watching your performance on videotape, you should quickly identify your weaknesses and strengths. You will improve with practice.

Preparing for Spontaneity

Following are some tips for taking the terror out of impromptu speaking:

1: Analyze Your Audience

Think hard about your audience members. Make sure you ask yourself who they are, what they care about, and what is in it for them. Once you know the specific characteristics of your listeners, you will be able to keep their attention long enough to persuade them.

2: Identify Your Communications Objective

Even if you have just a few seconds to prepare, decide what specific and measurable outcome you want to achieve as a result of your communication. Examples of good communication objectives are: I want the VP of sales to agree to meet with me again in one week; I want three volunteers to take on this assignment; I want Ted to champion this idea in the California office. Avoid communication objectives that are vague or too broad.

3: Stay Focused on Your Message

It is said that Henry Kissinger once opened a press conference by saying, "Does anyone have any questions for my answers?" This is exactly the right way to approach any impromptu speaking opportunity. When you are asked to make an impromptu presentation, or when you are answering questions during Q & A, think of it as another opportunity to make a case for your objectives.

4: Structure Your Response

When making impromptu comments or answering difficult questions, give an overview of what you plan to say before you begin your explanation. This is helpful to those audience members who didn't hear the question. It also gives you time to think. For example, "You've asked a good question about the ROI, and I plan to address this concern in a few minutes. First, for those of you who may not be familiar with our approach, I'd like to outline the rationale for change."

5: Don't Leave Anyone Out

Whether it's an audience of seven or 70 people, address your comments to the entire group. One of the biggest mistakes a speaker can make is to leave out members of the audience during Q & A. Refrain from the natural impulse to talk to the questioner or to the decision maker alone. This can engender bad feelings among the rest of the audience. For example, one company president recently severed a long-standing business relationship with a consultant because in meetings the consultant routinely focused on the person whom she perceived to be the decision maker. Eventually, she offended the wrong person and lost an important client.

6: Always Be Polite

If you are rude or impatient during Q & A, the audience will sympathize with the questioner. If you lose the sympathy of an audience, you will lose a powerful persuasion tool. This is one of the toughest messages to get through to young executives, who pride themselves on being "tough" and "brutally honest." Don't lower yourself to the level of a difficult questioner by saying something like, "So, exactly what's your point? I didn't hear a question in there." It is better to segue back to your main idea. "Tom, your anecdote certainly seems contrary to the point I was making, and I'm sure there are other objections; however, I want to focus on the general trends that we have uncovered through our research."

For most of us, the challenge of impromptu speaking hits home during the questions that follow the talk itself. Fortunately, most of the time audiences are kind and questioners seek clarification. Sometimes, questions are not straightforward and can be difficult to answer. Once in a while, people don't have your best interests at heart.

Difficult questions tend to fall into three categories: (1) unclear questions, (2) questions framed in a limited way, and (3) "I don't know" questions.

Unclear questions. Some questions are confusing because of their structure or word choice. The questioner may throw in vague phrases such as "this notion," "your plan," or "it." Other unclear questions refer to broad issues that can't be addressed in a limited time.

Begin by restating unclear questions. If the question is too broad, point out what part of the topic you plan to clarify and why. Vague language, such as the use of "this plan" or "it" should be defined. When several questions are strung together, separate them logically and decide which questions you will choose to answer. Remember that you are in charge of the flow of conversation.

Type of Leading Question	Strategy
Forced Choice Question: "What is more important to you, integrity or profits?"	Don't allow yourself to be restricted by an either/or choice. You can point out that *both* integrity and profits are important.
Hypothetical Question: "If earnings fall by 6% or more, will you take action?"	Whenever a question starts with "assume" or "if," you can refuse to speculate. Don't get pulled into a question that you don't want to answer.
Empty Chair Question: "Can you tell us what will be done at the top to address this crisis?"	It's best not to speak on behalf of anyone else, unless you are a spokesperson. When asked to comment on another executive's plans, it's safer to make it clear that you are speaking from your own vantage point.
Leading Question (with a false preface): "Since layoffs are inevitable, when will you be making the announcement?"	When the preface is false, recast the question. "If you are asking me whether or not layoffs are inevitable, the answer is no."
Emotionally Charged Question: "Frankly, this plan sounds like another one of your crazy schemes."	Refrain from taking the bait. You don't need to defend yourself. Restate your main points and move on.

Leading questions. Leading questions are meant to limit or restrict the speaker in some way. See the table for examples of five types of leading questions and strategies for not getting tripped up by them.

"I don't know" questions. There are times when you simply don't know the answer, or you need time to think. Never hazard a guess unless it's extremely clear that it's a guess. Better to say, "I don't know." It's a good idea to suggest where the person can find the answer or offer to find out the answer for them.

Impromptu speaking is never easy, but effective preparation builds confidence. That's the secret. You never know when you'll be put to the challenge.

For Further Reading

Guide to Presentations by Mary Munter and Lynn Russell (2002, Prentice Hall)

Reprint C0112C

Strengthening Your Presentation with Powerful Tools and Techniques

• • •

In addition to careful preparation and adroit delivery, an array of potent tools and techniques can help you further strengthen your presentations. The articles in this section introduce several—including additional suggestions for vanquishing stage fright and tips for avoiding common mistakes while using graphics during your talk.

Several articles also explain how to appeal to a broad range of listeners' learning styles—auditory, kinesthetic, and visual—and ways to use your own body language to reinforce your message and engage your audience more deeply. The concluding article provides 10 easy-to-remember guidelines to keep in mind as you contemplate your next presentation.

Six Ways to Overcome Your Fear of Public Speaking

• • •

Mike Grenby

Almost everyone fears public speaking to some degree, and no wonder. It's inherently frightening because it involves the risk of exposure in front of others—one of our most primal, deep-seated fears. It's the fear that you won't know what to say or how to say it, the fear of the unknown, and the fear of being judged by others, all rolled into one.

Standard treatment for *glossophobia*, as this condition is formally known, involves gradually lessening the fear. Those undergoing treatment typically begin with sessions in which they imagine giving a talk and slowly build up to the real thing.

But what if you don't have the time to devote to that gentle and rather lengthy process? Then it's time to take a radically different approach, one that uses techniques that are both radical, and, well, different.

> Once you experience the sensation of reduced adrenaline in a presentation-like setting, your body learns that it is possible to stand up in front of others and get over your panic.

For example, one public-speaking coach gathers his frightened clientele in a bar and has them bash bar stools with rolled-up newspapers while singing "Happy Birthday." Those who survive this exercise often find that they become confident speakers. Why? Because in comparison with what they've just done in public, delivering a speech or presentation before others now seems easy.

Before going into the details of this and other techniques, it's useful to understand the problem in a little more detail. Almost everyone experiences a little rush of fear, and a consequent adrenaline surge, at the prospect of public speaking. That heightened level of adrenaline helps most of us perform at peak level.

But for those who dread public speaking, the fear and the adrenaline rush can be overwhelming. All the knowledge in the world about how to prepare an effective presentation, all the time and effort devoted to preparing a brilliant PowerPoint or multimedia presentation, will come to naught if fear comes to the fore.

So get together a group of those in your workplace who particularly fear public speaking and try some of these proven techniques for vanquishing that fear.

1: Bashing a Bar (or Other) Stool

Use a rolled-up newspaper or hard foam water noodle for bashing. The group should applaud wildly—with whistles and supportive yelling—as each person goes up to the stool. Hit the stool to make as much noise as possible while yelling motivational slogans, or simply: "My name is _____. I feel just great and my presentation today is going to be fantastic!" As a change of pace and to add a personal note, also include phrases like: "What really bugs me is _____," or "When I go home I like to _____," or "My favorite food is _____."

The point is twofold and surprisingly subtle: The exercise works because bashing channels your adrenaline into physical release. And the simple act of yelling allows you to focus on the physical rather than the intellectual job of worrying about what you're going to say next.

Once you experience the sensation of reduced adrenaline in a presentation-like setting, your body learns that it is possible to stand up in front of others and get over your panic. And that's the first step toward confident public speaking.

2: Tabletop Poetry

A few days before the training session, ask participants to bring a poem they will recite, either from memory or by reading it (maximum: 15 lines). Each person stands on a low table in front of the group to deliver the poem. The poetry individuals choose often provides further personal insights—again, a good way to promote group bonding and spirit.

Here, the point is to take away the burden of having to make up your own material. Many people with deep anxiety about public speaking find that the fear comes in part from having to make something up. This exercise releases you from that burden.

3: Happy/Sad Nursery Rhymes

Proclaim the same verse of a nursery rhyme first with exaggerated humor and then with exaggerated sorrow.

The point here is to stretch your emotional range, which both relaxes you and makes you more charismatic. And, again, once you've done something like this in public, simply talking becomes easier.

4: Three-Way Sayings

Repeat the same sentence—e.g., "Turn out the lights," "Tell me how you feel," "What can I do for you?"—first in an angry tone, then in a puzzled tone, and then with exaggerated politeness.

Repeat the exercise, this time embellishing each sentence to emphasize the different modes. The purpose of the exercise is to stretch your emotional range, making you more expressive in public.

5: Simultaneous Debates

Participants pair off and select a topic for debate. When their turn comes around, the two stand up and start debating simultaneously, trying to drown out each other.

After 30 seconds, they reverse positions and take the opposite side of the topic—again, debating simultaneously.

If someone's focusing on simply trying to be heard over the other person's din, she won't have time to be nervous.

6: Singing "Happy Birthday"

Perhaps the most dreaded of all the exercises, this one will really stretch your comfort zone. Turn to others in the group and sing: "Happy birthday to you, / Happy birthday to you, / Happy birthday Mr./Ms. _____, / Happy birthday to you."

The audience should shout encouragement and applaud loudly. Once again, the point is not to be good, but to get over the fear of singing in public. Then speaking in public will seem simple by comparison.

The bottom line is that less fear can lead to more effective presentations.

—————————

Reprint C0303E

Presentations 101

Don't Make These Common Mistakes

• • •

John Clayton

Inexperienced presenters make two kinds of mistakes: the intelligent kind that all of us must work through, and the kind that is so obvious you just shake your head in disbelief.

Let's deal with the obvious ones first:

- **READING FROM A SCRIPT.** There's no faster way to lose your audience's attention. Instead, look up and establish a personal connection with the audience.

- **HIDING AT THE BACK OF THE ROOM OR BEHIND A PODIUM.** Let the audience see you and your body language.

- **IGNORING TIME CONSTRAINTS.** Don't try to give a 30-minute speech in a five-minute slot.

- **GOING OFF ON TANGENTS.** Anecdotes can be powerful tools; just be sure to keep them relevant to your point.

Then there are the mistakes that require more sophisticated responses.

1: Not Knowing Your Audience

In any communication task, you must understand what your audience needs to know. Your first step—long before you walk into the room—is to ask who the audience is and how they will use the information you provide. Then you can structure your presentation around those needs: pluses and minuses of a proposed strategy, overview of a new software package, or potential applications of the recent research.

In presentations, unlike in other forms of communication, your audience can and will give immediate feedback. Thus, the best presentations are interactive. At its most basic, interactivity comes in the form of a question or discussion time. More sophisticated—and usually more effective—are exercises that focus audience activity on key issues. For example, get your audience to design solutions to real problems that they are facing.

You can also use interactivity to fine-tune some details. For example, a written report might include the caveat "We assume you are familiar with single-entry accounting." But now you don't have to assume. Instead, ask, "Is everyone here familiar with single-entry accounting?" Don't forget to look around for their answers—and seek out the hesitant facial expressions of those who hate to admit their ignorance.

2: Failing to Grab Your Listeners' Attention

The audience arrives wondering: *Why should we care? Why is this important?* So, rather than jumping straight into the history of federal housing on Indian reservations, start by describing the current housing crisis. You get your listeners' minds working (*How did this come about? How can we solve it?*) in ways that give them context for the historical discussion.

Usually the easiest way to hook the audience is to describe the problem you set out to solve—though if the audience is familiar with it, make the description brief. Other successful "grabbers" can be anecdotes ("When I opened a can of our company's dog food last week, I discovered . . .") or surprising facts ("Over half of our customers expect to buy a DVD player within the next six months").

3: Neglecting to Provide a Road Map

Once you've gotten the audience interested, they start wondering, "Where are we going?" If the terrain is complicated, they may need a road map. A "Table of Contents" slide will help them understand what you want to do. As you start each new section of the outline, return to that slide to help your audience understand where they are, where they've been, and where they're going.

If your outline is simple, don't waste precious time on lengthy explanations. Still, you may want to describe in one sentence what the audience will learn. "By the end of today's presentation, I hope you will understand how online buying is shaping the industry, who the major players are, and where we should invest to compete."

4: Presenting Without Visual Aids

The five senses provide different pathways to people's brains. Your presentation should transmit information to your audience through these multiple pathways. Effects on smell, touch, and taste may be difficult to create—but visual aids are easy and powerful.

For many concepts—including relationships, flows, and spatial organization—we think visually. We have diagrams, charts, and maps in our heads. Why should you translate them into words and force your audience to translate them back to visuals?

Visual aids also trigger emotional responses (that's why advertisers show attractive, happy people using their products). We are especially drawn to pictures of other people. So, for example, if you are proposing strategies to improve employee satisfaction, or if you are commending individuals such as this month's sales leaders, use pictures to enhance the person-to-person aspects of communication.

> We have diagrams, charts, and maps in our heads. Why should you translate them into words and force your audience to translate them back to visuals?

By contrast, text-based visuals are barely better than no visuals at all. Because people can read faster than you can talk, they find nothing more boring than looking at a text-heavy slide as you read it aloud word-for-word. Visual aids should have objects, pictures, or diagrams combined with words; their effect should reinforce without repeating what you say aloud.

Similarly, visuals are usually best on a screen, not a handout. When you use a handout, people look at it instead of at you. You lose the audience focus and group dynamic. Handouts are good for listing procedures or providing properly spelled Web site addresses. But never hand out an article providing additional background—some people will read the handout instead of listening to you, and most will throw it away unread. Instead, let those who are interested come get it at the end of the presentation.

5: Using Visuals That Don't Relate to Your Message

Just as each paragraph you write should have a point, so should each visual aid. You express a paragraph's point in the topic sentence; you express a visual aid's point in its title. Why am I looking at this picture of smiling people? A title should tell me: "This initiative will increase employee satisfaction." Your words should also integrate with the visual, perhaps including phrases such as "As you can see on the slide. . . ."

Too often, a presenter will display a dense table of numbers, perhaps copied from another source. Which numbers should I look at? What trend do they illustrate? You should design and edit your visual aids in much the same way you format and edit a document—continually thinking about the effect on the audience. Should key numbers in this table be boldfaced? Should it be a pie chart or stacked-bar chart instead? By asking such questions, you continually compare your visual aid to the message you want it to convey.

6: Not Letting Visual Aids Do Their Work

Presenters make fascinating mistakes with visual aids:

- Blocking the screen with their bodies

- Talking to the screen rather than the audience

- Putting slides on an overhead projector upside-down—and never noticing

- Displaying a slide for ten seconds or less—not enough time for its message to sink in

Since you spend so much time developing an effective slide, make sure you let it do its work while you do yours. Practice to make the following physical actions become second nature:

- Stand where most of the audience can see both you and the screen

- Glance at each slide to make sure it's correct, then turn to address the audience

- As you speak, check your audience's faces to see that the slide has registered with them

7: Presenting Without Passion

Despite an ever-growing array of communication options, presentations remain essential to the business world. Why? In part, a presentation allows interaction between audience and presenter, and among audience members who can develop team spirit. But mainly, a presentation is an in-person experience. It's not just your words and visuals that make your presentation, but *you*. The audience will judge your credibility, substance, and passion—and they've come to the presentation because they can best make those judgments in person.

When you stand up in front of a crowd, you must believe that you're telling them something important. When the audience feels your trust and faith in the topic—if you have been effective in communicating it—you pass the implicit test they came to this room to give you. Your presentation succeeds.

Reprint C0011B

Presentations That Appeal to All Your Listeners

The Three Learning Styles and Levels

● ● ●

Many people are familiar with the three learning styles, typically referred to as the visual, auditory, and kinesthetic. But few have connected them with the crucial levels of learning that we all need to employ before we can truly know something—the intellectual, the emotional, and the physical. And fewer still apply them regularly to presentations. Is it any wonder, then, that most business presentations are only half-engaging and are quickly forgotten?

Picture the typical presentation. One of your colleagues is reporting the last quarter's results. She stands up in front of the group, turns on the overhead projector or her computer, and cues up the first slide. A sea of words and numbers greets your weary eyes. She then launches into reading every word on the screen. You shift in your chair, trying to get comfortable. As slide after slide winks by, and your colleague continues to drone on in a flat, uninflected voice, you gradually sink into an all-too-familiar semi-stupor. At the end you shake yourself, tell the speaker she did a good job, and walk out of the meeting room wondering to yourself what the point of the exercise really was.

The Three Learning Styles

How can we apply the three learning styles and levels to this doleful scene?

Visual Learning

Like most presenters, your colleague thinks she has appealed to the visual learner by using slides. But most business slides are covered with words, and what visual learners need is pictures. What's more, they learn best from simple pictures. So connect your key concepts visually to triangles, circles, squares, and the like. Don't get fancy. It's simply not necessary, and it doesn't promote learning. In addition to pictures, you can use graphic illustrations, tables and charts, and video for variety—but keep in mind that simpler is usually better.

Auditory Learning

You reach auditory learners through talk—but certain kinds of talk work better than others. Storytelling is probably the best approach. Parables and anecdotes will appeal to this kind of learner and be stored most directly into the memory. In addition, you can employ discussion groups, debates, question and answer sessions, and the like—anything that gets people talking in ways that are more connected to story than the usual discursive style of business speeches.

Kinesthetic Learning

Research shows that 30% to 40% of people are visual learners, 20% to 30% are auditory learners, and 30% to 50% are kinesthetic, meaning they learn best through physical activity. It is this last group that is most often neglected in business presentations. So much of the business world appeals to the head, not the body, and presentations are rarely exceptions to this dismal rule. The key here is to get your listeners doing something, practicing what you're preaching. Get them involved early and often through role-playing, games, working with models, even creating charts and physical representations of what you want them to learn.

For example, you can increase your listeners' energy enormously at the opening of a speech simply by having them stand up and shout something appropriate or fun. It's corny, but it works. That's because you have appealed to the kinesthetics in the audience.

The Three Levels of Learning

Now that you've got your listeners learning properly, how do you make your presentations memorable? By engaging the whole person, whether she is a visual, auditory, or kinesthetic learner, using all three levels of individual learning.

> If you convey a clear, strong message, the audience will respond clearly and strongly.

To put it simply, a good presentation must go beyond the intellectual level and directly bring in the subject's emotional component. How should your listeners feel about what you are saying? How do *you* feel about the topic? What is the emotional journey that your presentation takes the listener on? Is it coherent—or is it unexamined?

Unless you are clear about the emotional story you're telling, you can't expect to be able to communicate it. And your listeners won't form an emotional response to what you are saying if you haven't communicated your own. Audiences look to the speaker first for guidance about the emotional importance of the topic in deciding how they feel themselves.

In short, if you convey a clear, strong message, the audience will respond clearly and strongly. If you are fuzzy, the audience will respond fuzzily.

Similarly, you need to appeal to the physical level of learning if you are going to drive a message home to your listeners. When you're delivering a key message, get the audience to do something physical. Whether it's turning to a neighbor and repeating something to them, standing up and reciting a mnemonic device, or some other physical action, the activity will reinforce the underlying message.

Finally, here are some general tips for making sure that you are addressing all of the learning styles and levels in your presentations:

Allow for self-learning. Businesspeople like to be active. They are also adults. Let them do as much of the work of the presentation as possible, and they'll take it to heart more thoroughly.

Use their experience. Businesspeople enjoy bringing their own experience into the room. This method allows them to use the learning style most comfortable for them, and all the learning levels.

Use their motivation. Tell them what is in it for them. Frame the material you're presenting from their point of view. Why should they care about the topic at hand? If you begin with that, you'll enlist their help early on in getting your message across.

Give them a problem to solve. Businesspeople are problem-solvers. They are paid to be good at it. If you phrase your messages in terms of problems that they would like to solve, you'll involve them much more strongly.

For Further Reading

The Presentations Kit: 10 Steps for Selling Your Ideas by Claudyne Wilder (1994, John Wiley & Sons)

Turning Training into Learning: How to Design and Deliver Programs That Get Results by Sheila W. Furjanic and Laurie A. Trotman (2000, AMACOM)

99% Inspiration: Tips, Tales & Techniques for Liberating Your Business Creativity by Bryan W. Mattimore (1993, AMACOM)

Games Trainers Play: Experiential Learning Exercises by John W. Newstrom and Edward E. Scannell (1989, McGraw-Hill)

Creativity Games for Trainers: A Handbook of Group Activities for Jumpstarting Workplace Creativity by Robert Epstein (1996, McGraw-Hill)

Reprint C0006B

How to Make Even Weak Speeches Great

The Key Is Using Your Physical Presence to Create Trust

• • •

Nick Morgan

Which is more important, the speaker or the speech? In other words, is it better for the audience to have great content delivered in a mediocre fashion, or mediocre content delivered extremely well?

Orators and their audiences have pondered this conundrum for 2,500 years or more, yet in truth we've known the answer for just as long. We simply don't want to admit it, because the truth makes us squirm a little.

Quintilian, one of the first great classical experts on oration, gave the first answer, and it has stood for the ages, if uncomfortably. "For my own part," he argues in his *Institutio,* XI 3.5–6, "I would not hesitate to assert that a mediocre speech supported by all the power of delivery will be more impressive than the best speech unaccompanied by such power."

There you have it. This answer makes us uncomfortable because it seems cynical to acknowledge the primacy of delivery over content. It means that we, as audiences, are more susceptible to the emotions and excitement of the moment than we would like to admit. We prize the picture of ourselves as rational creatures who are swayed by logic, not passion. To admit the alternative seems to open the floodgates to hucksterism, slick oratory, and fast-talking salespeople. To that other almost as ancient (and rhetorical) question, "Would you buy a used car from so-and-so?" we are forced to answer, "Yes, if so-and-so was really good."

And yet to experience this discomfort is to look at the question in the wrong way. The question really should be, "What moves an audience to action? Fair words or fair face?" And the answer is that audiences are moved to action by speakers they trust. Once a speech is fully launched, a successful presenter can feel the audience deciding to trust her. The audience simultaneously relaxes—because it knows it is not wasting its time—and pays attention—because it is confirmed in its original decision to attend the speech. A kinesthetic bond develops between the audience and the speaker. It is this kinesthetic moment that fundamentally determines the success or failure of a presentation.

Kinesthetics is the awareness of where you are in space in relation to other people. It is the single most important skill to master as a presenter.

> A speaker has only the first five minutes of a speech to get over her stage fright. After that, nervousness becomes a distinct liability.

Why should this be so? Think of the issue from the audience's point of view. It is simply smart, not cynical, to try to judge underlying motivations before deciding to trust a presenter. At this level, emotions do become paramount. Audiences should try to read the nonverbal communications of speakers precisely because it is here that issues of trust are best decided. Most people are not great liars (or actors). Speakers are no exception. Under the influence of adrenaline, most presenters resort to instinctive gestures conveying nonverbal communication learned over a lifetime. It is at this level that audiences take the measure of their speakers—and it is right that they should do so. It's not terribly easy to work up a slick sales pitch, but it is even harder to create a great presentation out of mediocre material that you don't believe.

Audiences understand this, and so they take the measure of the presenter at a mostly unconscious level, deciding whether or not to trust her (and buy the message) based on the speaker's ability to connect with the audience in a way that appears sincere, straightforward, and open.

Following are some tips to ensure that your kinesthetic performance doesn't get in the way of connecting with your audience—and in fact creates an opportunity for a true kinesthetic bond to develop between you and them.

1: Get over your nervousness—fast

Most speakers spend the first few minutes of a presentation working out the worst of their nerves. It's something that audiences expect, and they're willing to cut the presenter some slack at the opening. An audience expects a speaker to warm to her task, however, and to begin to relax a few minutes into the speech. If the speaker remains nervous, the audience will begin to find that nervousness a barrier to comprehension of the rest of the speech, and to trust. Unfortunately, that means that a speaker only has at most the first five minutes of a speech to get over her stage fright. After that, nervousness becomes a distinct liability.

The reason is that the audience is eager to decide whether or not to trust a presenter, and so it interprets the speaker's behavior as meaningful *to the audience,* even if the speaker is merely struggling with nerves.

So it's up to you to figure out how to reach a plateau of relative comfort quickly. For some, mental imagining—to counteract the doom scenarios we all play out in our heads—seems to help. For others, breathing and self-directed pep talks are efficacious. For all of us, preparation and practice are essential. If you're tempted to wing it—don't. It may work some of the time, but it won't always be enough, and there is no feeling worse than that of losing an audience halfway through a talk because you suddenly realize you don't really know what you're talking about.

2: It's not what you do, it's what they see

Audiences interpret behavior as meaningful to them. So, for example, if you're feeling cold in front of an audience because the air conditioning in the room is turned down too far, resist the temptation to cross your arms. Audiences will probably take this gesture to mean that you're feeling defensive, even if they're cold themselves.

Spend some time thinking through the ways in which your audience is likely to interpret your standard repertoire of gestures. If you don't know what they are, get a close friend to tell you—or arrange to have yourself videotaped. Many people back away from an audience, for example, if emotions threaten to become heated. Someone will ask a strongly worded question, say, and the speaker will retreat to the safety of the podium. Audiences will almost always interpret this gesture as a sign of unwillingness to engage in the important issues, or even as simple fear. So, if questioners turn up the heat on you, don't back down. Get in their personal space, maintain your cool, and answer the question.

3: Above all, remember the audience's need to connect with you

The easiest way to get a reading on what another person is really thinking—indeed the only way we're truly comfortable with—is when that person is having a one-on-one conversation with us. As a speaker, you need to respect that need in each individual member of your audience. But how can you manage this feat when you're talking to a hundred people—or a thousand?

You can't, literally. But you can do the next best thing. You can connect personally with a few members of the audience by moving in close to them—between four feet and two feet away—and allowing those members of the audience to stand in proxy to the whole. Audiences are willing to accept this second-best solution. What they are not willing to accept is the sincerity of someone who begins a speech behind the podium and never leaves it to try to move closer to them. If you are one of those speakers who can't bear to leave the safety of the space behind the podium, either get over your fears or leave the speaking to someone else. In today's casual rhetorical atmosphere, traditional podium speaking is simply no longer adequate.

> Make your content and your actions cohere by moving toward your listeners at key moments and away from them when you want to signal a pause or change of topic.

Now, it's not enough just to move randomly toward various audience members as you're talking through your slides. Because you raise the energy in the room and focus attention on yourself when you move in close to an audience member, you need to pick the right moment. If you're not saying something important then, your kinesthetic message and your content will be at odds. This sets up a battle between your listeners' conscious deciphering of the content and their largely unconscious reading of your motivations. Your listeners will begin to wonder what's really important—they may simply interpret what you say while you're standing close to them as the main points. If those aren't the main points, you'll confuse your listeners.

Remember the TV show *Columbo*? The rumpled detective would wear down his suspect (almost always the guilty party) by working his way through a long list of mumbled and often irrelevant questions. Finally, he would start to move away, and the guilty party would breathe a sigh of relief and begin to relax. Then Columbo would turn back and say something like, "One more thing. What was the color of the tie you were wearing that day?" Columbo was signaling that his question was less important than it really was by his kinesthetic distance from the criminal. The result was that the criminal was more likely to tell him the truth in an unguarded moment.

There, the kinesthetic message and the content are deliberately at variance because Columbo wants to trick the truth out of the guilty party. Speakers need to use the same wisdom about kinesthetic messages but in a more positive way. Rather than tricking your audience, make your content and your actions cohere by moving toward your listeners at key moments and away from them when you want to signal a pause or change of topic.

Good kinesthetic speaking means making your content and your delivery consistent with one another. Far too many business speakers lurk behind podiums or wander around the public space in front of an audience, wondering why they can't seem to connect with their listeners. The answer has been available for 2,500 years, as long as people have been presenting—and struggling to do it more successfully.

For Further Reading

"The Kinesthetic Speaker: Putting Action into Words" by Nick Morgan (April 2001, *Harvard Business Review*)

Reprint C0108B

The Ten Commandments of Presentations

• • •

You've just been promoted. Congratulations. You gave yourself a weekend to enjoy the feeling, and now Monday has arrived with its new responsibilities. You have to address your new team. Public speaking has always been nerve-wracking for you, but this time is special. You really want to make a good impression right out of the starting gate, and the team needs to be charged up for the race ahead. For the first time in your career, the stakes are beginning to seem high.

It's time to learn what really makes a successful presentation. Forget the rules you learned in high-school debate or college communication classes. It's time for the rubber to hit the public speaking road. It's time for the Ten Commandments of Presentations.

Thou shalt respect thine audience

The only reason to feel nervous is to use that adrenaline to speak with more energy. Because presentations aren't about you, the speaker. They're about the audience. Good public speaking begins with respecting the audience. The moment you realize that it's not what you say that counts in the end, but what the audience hears, you will be on the road toward becoming a great speaker. And you'll forget about your own nervousness.

How does that actually work in practice? You need to shift your focus from your own symptoms to the audience's reception of your presentation. Concentrate on them. Make eye contact for five or six seconds with people in the front, left and right, and the back. Watch their body language. Are they engaged? Have they checked out? If they have, stop and ask them what's on their mind—in the context of the presentation. Take their "temperature." Move in close to selected parts of the audience, as close as four feet. You'll get them back.

Thou shalt keep thy slides to an absolute minimum

The ugly truth is that most speakers use their slides as a crutch to help them limp through a lame presentation, or as an outline for themselves because they haven't adequately prepared for the talk. Rarely are slides actually

157

used for the purpose they are best suited to: visually reinforcing key points in a presentation.

An enormous number of business people watch an even greater number of slides day in and day out because speakers have half-learned a dubious wisdom, that there are "visual learners" out there, and that a large number of slides will help them learn. It's time to face the reality. Yes, one theory has it that there are three kinds of learners—visual, auditory, and kinesthetic. Yes, those visual learners do like pictures. They also like good metaphors, videos, broad overviews, and enthusiastic gestures. What they don't like is one slide after another packed with words—and that's what most speakers offer their audiences. No audience, and especially not one packed with visual learners, likes slides with more than about six lines of text on them. And the fewer of those the better. They like pictures. Think back to your last talk. How many lines of text did you use? How many actual pictures? Microsoft clip art does not count. It looks cheap, and everyone knows you threw it in at the last minute. Don't use it.

Thou shalt not tell thine audience how nervous thou art, but thou shalt tell it how thou feelest

All public speakers want to be charismatic. But charisma comes from having something true and heartfelt to put on the line in front of your audience. Charisma comes from the honest expression of emotion when something real is at stake. To be a successful speaker, you have to confront yourself, perhaps for the first time, and decide who you are and what you stand for. When you are able to share that with an audience, they will stand up and cheer. Because you will have forgotten about yourself and your nervousness and given something real to them.

Thou shalt know what time it is at all times

The attention span of an audience diminishes rapidly as the day goes on. By dinner time, it's 12 minutes or less. If called upon to give an after-dinner speech, especially if alcohol has been served, keep it to seven minutes if you can. You're competing with the audience's gastric juices, and gastric juices always win.

Similarly, respect the time period set aside for your presentation. If you've agreed to speak for an hour, go for 45 or 50 minutes and stop for questions. Never run long. Nobody ever asked a public speaker for an encore. And don't keep people waiting for a meal. If you're the last speaker before lunch, end a little early. They're thinking about their salads anyhow.

Thou shalt learn from thy masters

Study the speeches of the great orators of our day. There is almost always an ethical dimension to their messages.

They first tell their audiences why they should strive for some goal or attempt to accomplish some task. Then they tell them how. And then they give their audiences something to do, either rhetorically or actually. Most great political speeches end with either a rhetorical charge to the audience ("Ask not what your country can do for you—ask what you can do for your country") or a chance for the audience to chant something back to the speaker (Jesse Jackson's "I am . . . somebody"). This device moves the audience from passive to active, and helps bring it to the cause. Give your audiences something to do, or they will remain passive observers.

Thou shalt neither read nor memorize a speech word for word

The fastest way to kill an audience is to read to them from a text at a podium. Both the text and the podium separate the speaker from his listeners. Why should an audience have to work hard to bridge the gap? But memorizing a speech so you can leave the notes behind can be equally deadening. Unless you're an accomplished actor, you probably can't recite lines with anything like the life they need to keep an audience engaged. Some speakers find it useful to memorize the beginning and ending of a presentation, in order to begin and end error-free. But it is better to adopt a conversational tone throughout, speak from notes, and practice until you're comfortable with the material.

Thou shalt remember the difference between flirtation and presentation

Many presenters groom themselves unconsciously during their talks because of nervousness. If you're prone to this behavior, make yourself follow a simple rule: when speaking, keep your hands below your neck (and above your waist). Grooming is a universally understood sign of sexual interest in all primates. Thus, you will send out a confusing double message to your listeners if you groom. On the one hand, you will be saying, "Listen to me, what I have to say is important." And on the other hand, your grooming will be saying (subconsciously), "Aren't I cute? Don't listen to what I'm saying. Look at me." The result is that the audience will not take you seriously and neither you nor your audience will know why.

Thou shalt give credit where credit is due

If you borrow other people's thoughts or words, credit them. Better yet, quote them accurately. Judicious quotations can add luster to a talk. A speech or presentation is a public occasion, and you are expected to live up to public standards of honesty, fairness, and tact. Moreover, check your facts and your data for accuracy. Many a good speech has been derailed by that single question from the back of the room showing the speaker's facts to be wrong.

161

Your listeners grant you credibility to start with. They have voted with their feet; they have come to hear you talk. Thus, initially at least, they are hoping that you will succeed. The credibility they have given you is yours to lose. Don't tell your audience too little or too much. Both tactics undermine credibility. Give your listeners enough supporting data to illustrate but not to exhaust. And make sure it is accurate.

Thou shalt have a positive message

Most people respond to a speaker who has a scapegoat for the audience's problems. But an audience will not listen for long if that is all a speaker has. Don't get up to speak in front of a group of people unless you have something positive to offer. Listeners give you their trust provisionally: they assume that you are an authority, that you do have something to say. Like credibility, trust is yours to lose. The fastest way to lose it is to give only negative messages. Listeners are looking to you for two things, primarily: to identify their problems, and to solve them. By doing both, you cement the bond of trust between you and them.

Thou shalt tell thine own story

There are two secrets for great public speaking: enjoying yourself, and telling a strong, coherent story. It is difficult to accomplish the former without having the latter. Take the time to develop a story that comes from your own thoughts and beliefs. If you're fundamentally telling someone else's tale, you'll never achieve that happy state where you and your listeners are as one, and you're all having a great time.

Follow these commandments, and with practice you'll become a speaker people turn to when they want to hear something significant and lasting. And remember, a presentation belongs to its listeners. If they don't get it, no communication has taken place, and everyone's time has been wasted.

Reprint C9907C

About the Contributors

Nick Morgan is a former editor at *Harvard Management Update*.

Michael Hattersley is a former contributor to *Harvard Management Communication Letter*.

John Daly is Liddell Professor in the College of Communication, University. Distinguished Teaching Professor, Texas Commerce Banc Shares Professor of Management, and Professor of Pharmacy.

Isa Engleberg is coauthor of *Working in Groups*.

Beverly Ballaro has taught language, literature, or writing courses at Yale, Cornell, and Wheelock College.

Richard Bierck is a freelance financial writer based in Princeton, N.J. His work has appeared in *U.S. News & World Report, Bloomberg Personal Finance,* and *Parade*.

Judith Humphrey is president of the Humphrey Group, a Toronto-based firm that specializes in executive speech training.

Cheryl Wiles is an independent speech coach based in the Boston area. She has taught workshops at Columbia Business School and is affiliated with Columbia's Executive program.

About the Contributors

Mike Grenby is an author, syndicated financial columnist, keynote speaker at money seminars and shows, and assistant professor of communications and media studies at Bond University in Gold Coast, Australia.

John Clayton is a writer and teacher at Rocky Mountain College in Billings, Montana.

Harvard Business Review Paperback Series

The Harvard Business Review Paperback Series offers the best thinking on cutting-edge management ideas from the world's leading thinkers, researchers, and managers. Designed for leaders who believe in the power of ideas to change business, these books will be useful to managers at all levels of experience, but especially senior executives and general managers. In addition, this series is widely used in training and executive development programs.

Books are priced at $19.95 U.S.
Price subject to change.

Title	Product #
Harvard Business Review **Interviews with CEOs**	3294
Harvard Business Review on **Advances in Strategy**	8032
Harvard Business Review on **Becoming a High Performance Manager**	1296
Harvard Business Review on **Brand Management**	1445
Harvard Business Review on **Breakthrough Leadership**	8059
Harvard Business Review on **Breakthrough Thinking**	181X
Harvard Business Review on **Building Personal and Organizational Resilience**	2721
Harvard Business Review on **Business and the Environment**	2336
Harvard Business Review on **Change**	8842
Harvard Business Review on **Compensation**	701X
Harvard Business Review on **Corporate Ethics**	273X
Harvard Business Review on **Corporate Governance**	2379
Harvard Business Review on **Corporate Responsibility**	2748
Harvard Business Review on **Corporate Strategy**	1429
Harvard Business Review on **Crisis Management**	2352
Harvard Business Review on **Culture and Change**	8369
Harvard Business Review on **Customer Relationship Management**	6994
Harvard Business Review on **Decision Making**	5572
Harvard Business Review on **Effective Communication**	1437

Title	Product #
Harvard Business Review on **Entrepreneurship**	9105
Harvard Business Review on **Finding and Keeping the Best People**	5564
Harvard Business Review on **Innovation**	6145
Harvard Business Review on **Knowledge Management**	8818
Harvard Business Review on **Leadership**	8834
Harvard Business Review on **Leadership at the Top**	2756
Harvard Business Review on **Leading in Turbulent Times**	1806
Harvard Business Review on **Managing Diversity**	7001
Harvard Business Review on **Managing High-Tech Industries**	1828
Harvard Business Review on **Managing People**	9075
Harvard Business Review on **Managing the Value Chain**	2344
Harvard Business Review on **Managing Uncertainty**	9083
Harvard Business Review on **Managing Your Career**	1318
Harvard Business Review on **Marketing**	8040
Harvard Business Review on **Measuring Corporate Performance**	8826
Harvard Business Review on **Mergers and Acquisitions**	5556
Harvard Business Review on **Motivating People**	1326
Harvard Business Review on **Negotiation**	2360
Harvard Business Review on **Nonprofits**	9091
Harvard Business Review on **Organizational Learning**	6153
Harvard Business Review on **Strategic Alliances**	1334
Harvard Business Review on **Strategies for Growth**	8850
Harvard Business Review on **The Business Value of IT**	9121
Harvard Business Review on **The Innovative Enterprise**	130X
Harvard Business Review on **Turnarounds**	6366
Harvard Business Review on **What Makes a Leader**	6374
Harvard Business Review on **Work and Life Balance**	3286

Management Dilemmas:
Case Studies from the Pages of Harvard Business Review

How often do you wish you could turn to a panel of experts to guide you through tough management situations? The Management Dilemmas series provides just that. Drawn from the pages of *Harvard Business Review,* each insightful volume poses several perplexing predicaments and shares the problem-solving wisdom of leading experts. Engagingly written, these solutions-oriented collections help managers make sound judgment calls when addressing everyday management dilemmas.

These books are priced at $19.95 U.S.
Price subject to change.

Title	Product #
Management Dilemmas: **When Change Comes Undone**	5038
Management Dilemmas: **When Good People Behave Badly**	5046
Management Dilemmas: **When Marketing Becomes a Minefield**	290X

Harvard Business Essentials

In the fast-paced world of business today, everyone needs a personal resource—a place to go for advice, coaching, background information, or answers. The Harvard Business Essentials series fits the bill. Concise and straightforward, these books provide highly practical advice for readers at all levels of experience. Whether you are a new manager interested in expanding your skills or an experienced executive looking to stay on top, these solution-oriented books give you the reliable tips and tools you need to improve your performance and get the job done. Harvard Business Essentials titles will quickly become your constant companions and trusted guides.

These books are priced at $19.95 U.S., except as noted.
Price subject to change.

Title	Product #
Harvard Business Essentials: **Negotiation**	1113
Harvard Business Essentials: **Managing Creativity and Innovation**	1121
Harvard Business Essentials: **Managing Change and Transition**	8741
Harvard Business Essentials: **Hiring and Keeping the Best People**	875X
Harvard Business Essentials: **Finance**	8768
Harvard Business Essentials: **Business Communication**	113X
Harvard Business Essentials: **Manager's Toolkit ($24.95)**	2896
Harvard Business Essentials: **Managing Projects Large and Small**	3213
Harvard Business Essentials: **Creating Teams with an Edge**	290X

The Results-Driven Manager

The Results-Driven Manager series collects timely articles from *Harvard Management Update* and *Harvard Management Communication Letter* to help senior to middle managers sharpen their skills, increase their effectiveness, and gain a competitive edge. Presented in a concise, accessible format to save managers valuable time, these books offer authoritative insights and techniques for improving job performance and achieving immediate results.

These books are priced at $14.95 U.S.
Price subject to change.

Readers of the Results-Driven Manager series find the following Harvard Business School Press books of interest.

If you find these books useful:	You may also like these:
Presentations That Persuade and Motivate	Working the Room (8199)
Face-to-Face Communications for Clarity and Impact	HBR on Effective Communication (1437) HBR on Managing People (9075)
Winning Negotiations That Preserve Relationships	HBR on Negotiation (2360) HBE Guide to Negotiation (1113)
Teams That Click	The Wisdom of Teams (3670) Leading Teams (3332)
Managing Yourself for the Career You Want	Primal Leadership (486X) Leading Quietly (4878) Leadership on the Line (4371)

How to Order

Harvard Business School Press publications are available worldwide from your local bookseller or online retailor.
You can also call

1-800-668-6780

Our product consultants are available to help you
8:00 a.m.–6:00 p.m., Monday–Friday, Eastern Time.
Outside the U.S. and Canada, call: 617-783-7450
Please call about special discounts for quantities greater than ten.

You can order online at

www.HBSPress.org